AF619399

The Long Dance Back

A Memoir of Survival and Returning to Life

by
Janette Mari

Published by Mari House Publications
Cover design by Kristin Villatuya

Some names and identifying details have been changed to protect privacy.

Content Warning

This memoir recounts real-life experiences that include violence, sexual assault, medical emergencies and other intense situations. Some passages may be upsetting or triggering. While these events were harrowing, this book also celebrates survival, resilience, and the courage it takes to reclaim your life. Reader discretion is advised.

ISBN: 979-8-9953195-0-4

Printed in the United States of America

First Edition

In Loving Memory of Peter Anderson

Peter Anderson was more than my editor. He was a wise and generous friend, a steady partner in this project, and a voice of encouragement during some of the hardest chapters of my life. His insight, warmth, and deep belief in this memoir helped shape its heart as much as its pages.

Peter passed away before the book was completed, yet his presence is woven through every chapter. His thoughtful guidance, patience, and gentle way of elevating my words continue to echo in this work. I carry immense gratitude for the time we shared and for the care he poured into this story.

This book is stronger because of him. This journey was lighter because of him. His memory lives on here, held with honor, respect, and love.

Forever in my heart.

TABLE OF CONTENTS

For Leonie,
my granddaughter, my light,
and the reason I found my way back from the darkness

ACKNOWLEDGEMENTS

This memoir would not exist without the incredible people who have stood beside me, reminding me again and again that I am never alone.

To my granddaughter, Leonie, your laughter is pure light in my life. You have taught me to celebrate each moment, no matter how small, and to find joy even after the darkest days.

To my daughters, Ashley and Kristin, you are my heart and my strength. Your love, patience, and unwavering support carried me through every storm and every chapter of this journey.

To my son-in-law, Ryan, thank you for your kindness, your steady strength, and for loving my daughter so well. I am deeply grateful for the calm and faithful presence you bring to our family.

To my son-in-law, Kris, and to his parents, Cindi and Iraj, and his sister, Ashlee, thank you for embracing me as your own. Your love, steadfast support, and the power of your prayers surrounded me during my most fragile moments. I felt them. I will always carry that with me.

To my sister-in-law, Ingrid, and my nephew, Josh, thank you for dropping everything, packing your bags, and standing by my side through each medical crisis. Your care, your presence, and your willingness to hold up my world when I could not stand on my own will stay with me forever.

To my siblings and their spouses — Jun; Jane and John; and Joji and Danny — your encouragement, love, and belief in me sustained me. Joji, your fierce advocacy during my writing journey kept me going when the words felt too heavy to lift.

To the doctors, nurses, and caregivers who held my hand, soothed my fears, and fought alongside me, you helped me survive. Your compassion made all the difference.

This story may have my name on the cover, but it was written with the love, strength, and faith of all of you—and by the grace of God, who carried me through it all.

PETER'S INTRODUCTION

A courageous woman's pursuit of meaning, healing, and joy, embracing life's hardships and triumphs with an open heart; her deep craving for friendship, love, and family intimacy; and her unwavering commitment to celebrate life, build businesses, overcome challenges, and find meaning in a world full of struggle and triumph.

My name is Peter Anderson. I am Janette's friend, interviewer, editor, and partner in this deeply personal project. A lifelong resident of Marin and San Francisco, an author and columnist, I've spent decades profiling public figures, including entertainers, politicians, and writers. Janette drew me in for an entirely different reason. She is a remarkable woman living quietly beneath the radar, yet brimming with life, empathy, and curiosity. She embodies carpe diem, embracing joy and hardship with equal openness, learning from them both, and meeting the world with a generous heart.

We met in an unlikely place, a San Francisco Giants fan site. Forums can be harsh and unforgiving, but Janette held her ground with intelligence, fairness, and what I call tough kindness. And yes, she is radiant. Beneath that warmth, I discovered a woman of depth and resilience, qualities this memoir reveals in full.

Her devotion to family and friends is extraordinary. She gives freely, navigates relationships with intention, and grows through her connections. Watching her live so fully has been inspiring, especially for someone like me who prefers the quiet role of observer.

Janette's childhood shaped her into a fighter. Life demanded perseverance early, yet she walks forward unspoiled by either hardship or success. People are drawn to her because she leads with authenticity, curiosity, and a willingness to show her whole self.

This memoir is her voice. My role has simply been to walk beside her, helping her bring that voice to the page with honesty and vulnerability. The story that follows is entirely hers—raw, unpolished, real, and filled with the courage to face her past and embrace her present.

Finally, I must thank her for her trust, especially through her recent health challenges. She faced them with prayer, perseverance, and immense courage. Her strength during those difficult months reminded me, again, of the remarkable woman at the center of this book.

Enough from me. This is her story, her words, her world. Enjoy.

PREFACE

Finding My Voice Again

I grew up in a Filipino household where emotions were quiet, expectations were high, and talking back was unthinkable. Family wasn't something you shared around a table; it was something you carried on your back. Heavy. Expected. Unspoken.

Love wasn't affectionately displayed. Warmth came in a full plate, not a hug. We didn't ask how your day was. We just kept going. In our house, vulnerability was weakness, and silence was survival.

Looking back, I see how much of my early life was shaped by what we didn't say. Yet even then, beneath all that quiet, a spark lived inside me. Small, but stubborn.

What I couldn't have imagined was how fiercely that spark would be tested. I would face two kidnappings, two near-death surgeries, a stroke, and a darkness so deep I didn't know if I wanted to keep living.

But through it all, that same flicker of hope refused to die. Every time life broke me open, I discovered another layer of strength, another piece of my voice.

This memoir is not just about what broke me; it's about what healed me. It's about faith, humor, and the small, defiant voice that kept whispering, *Keep going*. This is how I found my voice again, how I learned that even a whisper can save your life.

CHAPTER 1
I WAS AN UGLY DUCKLING

I didn't start out as an ugly duckling. As a toddler, I was undeniably adorable, with dark, curly hair, big curious eyes, and a bright smile that lit up my chubby little face. People would stop my mom in the streets to gush over me, calling me cutie, doll, angel. But somewhere between those picture-perfect baby years and the start of elementary school, something changed.

My second set of teeth came in way too big for my small face, and those big, curious eyes people used to gush over had morphed into something closer to big, bulging ones. Overnight, my once-round features transformed and stretched into something I didn't recognize. I didn't understand what was happening. I only knew that the mirror no longer smiled back the way it used to. Kids at school noticed too, giving me a new nickname, ugly duckling. At home, my brother had his own name for me, Popeyes. Both stuck harder than I ever wanted them to, and even today, they echo in the back of my mind.

I was born in Manila, Philippines, the middle child of five. My father, Dr. Alfredo Guevara, served in the U.S. Navy and rose to Chief Petty Officer before retiring. After his service, he used the GI Bill to attend dental school and became a dentist. My mother, Leonisa Padilla, was a strong-willed schoolteacher from Nueva Ecija. Before he met Mom, Dad had already adopted his niece, Daisy, as his own daughter. After Mom and Dad married, Joji came first, then Jun, then me, and finally Jane, the baby of the family.

Dad's military career had taken him across the globe, and one of the defining moments of his life was surviving the attack on Pearl Harbor on December 7, 1941. Recently, my siblings and I attended a ceremony awarding him the Congressional Gold Medal, a long-overdue recognition of his courage. Standing there, seeing his legacy honored, I felt the weight of history and the strength he passed down to all of us.

When he and Mom decided to build a future in America, he gave up his dental practice so he could leave first and get established. Practicing dentistry in the United States proved too difficult to continue, yet everyone still respectfully called him Dr. Guevara, a title he carried with quiet pride.

My parents met the old-fashioned way, at a dance. Dad was seventeen years older than her, already worldly and well-traveled from his time at sea. She was young, serious, and sharp. Something about her stilled him. Not long after they met, he wrote her a love letter. We didn't find it until years later, after he had passed and she was nearly ninety. It was tucked away with old documents, written in flowing script that time hadn't faded. It began simply: Dear Leonie. None of us had ever heard him call her that before. Whether it was a nickname or he simply forgot her name, we'll never know. But it stuck, the name, the moment, the quiet love between the lines.

When Mom passed, my daughters and I each had *Dear Leonie* tattooed on our forearms in Dad's handwriting. It was our way of carrying their story forward. Years later, when my granddaughter was born, she was named Leonie, an echo of that long-ago letter and a tribute to love that crossed oceans and generations.

Aside from our adopted sister Daisy, Joji was the oldest and clearly Dad's favorite. My brother, Alfredo Jr., known as Jun, came next. As the only son, he was practically untouchable. I arrived two years later, sandwiched in the middle. Middle children know the diplomatic zone, the forgotten seat at the family dinner table. Not the firstborn. Not the boy. Not the baby. I felt it deeply, though I didn't have the words for it then.

Six years after I was born came Jane, the youngest, the golden one. She could do no wrong. I could trip over thin air and get scolded; she could knock over a lamp and get a hug. Mom affectionately called her "the sweet mistake," born when she was forty and Dad was fifty-seven.

From the outside, we seemed like a typical Filipino-American immigrant family. Inside, it was more complicated. Jun was clearly Mom's favorite, and

I quickly learned that nothing I did could change that. I was often asked to do the "boy" chores, hauling trash, pulling weeds, doing the work no one else wanted. It felt like being overlooked and overburdened at the same time.

And then there was me, always in the middle, shrinking, questioning my worth, wondering where I belonged, not just in our family but in the world.

When I was just a year old, Dad sent for us to join him in America. He had retired from the Navy and was working at the Rincon Annex Post Office near San Francisco's Embarcadero. Daisy stayed in the Philippines for medical school, so it was just Joji, Jun, and me. Jane would be born later in the States. We moved into a small flat on Broderick Street in Pacific Heights, an area that would later become one of the city's most expensive neighborhoods, though it was anything but glamorous at the time.

I don't have many memories from our time there, but one has stayed with me all my life. It's just a moment, really, but it's etched into my heart. I had to be a young toddler. Mom was rocking me in her arms, singing "Sleep My Little Baby" in her soft, high-pitched voice. I can still see it, feel it, like it was just yesterday. The warmth of her body, the rhythm of her sway, the sound of her voice, comforting, safe, and pure. That one memory is all I can recall from our time on Broderick Street, but it has never left me.

CHAPTER 2
HAUNTED ON MOSCOW STREET

I've tried to recall a happy memory from Moscow Street, but the cramped two-bedroom house in the foggy hills might as well have been a haunted dollhouse. Mom and Dad had a bedroom. Jun usually had the second. Joji and I shared the living room sofa bed, limbs overlapping, blankets fought over, the steel bar digging into our backs. Mom's obsession with covering us up, with bandanas, layers, tights under skirts, and long sleeves even in spring, made us look like dolls from another era, boxed in under some invisible spotlight.

I think I was depressed before I even knew the word. Always in trouble for breathing too loud or blinking wrong. Being the middle child felt like no-man's-land: not old enough to be admired, not young enough to be adored. Jun was the golden boy, Joji was the star student and "little mom," and me? Furniture. If furniture cried, that was me.

Mom worked as a dietician at a hospital, starting her day long before dawn. One small perk of those early hours was that she often brought home deli ham for sandwiches and fresh glazed donuts, little treasures that briefly brightened the routine. Dad worked swing shift at the post office, so during the week he was almost a ghost in the house, leaving early afternoon and returning close to midnight. Weekends felt staged, with family outings to Playland, picnics, and occasional trips to relatives. Hollow, mechanical, lacking warmth.

Mom never learned to drive and flat-out refused, so Dad was her full-time chauffeur. The routine never changed. We weren't a close family. We coexisted. Survived, really.

Jun's favorite pastime was terrorizing me. Greatest hit? Rolling me up in an area rug like a human burrito. Arms pinned, chest compressed, breath slow and panicked. Screams tore through the house. I thrashed, twisted, helpless. Mom walked in and burst out laughing. Joji joined in. Apparently, my suffering was prime-time entertainment. I wondered if my mother even liked me, or if I'd been switched at birth with the family punching bag.

Joji wasn't exactly handing out sisterly love either. She often chased me with the vacuum cleaner, her weapon of choice. One night, she painted vivid, terrifying pictures: I'd be sucked into the vacuum, turned to dirt, thrown out with the trash. Legs pumped like pistons, arms flailed, zigzagging across the room in desperate, frantic patterns.

"Dance!" she commanded.

I twisted and jumped with every bit of energy I had. "But I'm getting tired!" I shouted, gasping over the roar of the machine. Heart thrashed like a caged animal. Dust coated my face, and my splintered hands scraped the floor. Joji's face twisted in delight, victorious, predatory. I couldn't breathe. I was prey, powerless. The hunter? My sister.

Another time, when Mom was pregnant with Jane, I was bursting with joy over the new crib. Momentarily peaceful, hopeful. Then Joji, in a terrifying mood, chased me through the house with an iron. Cord snapping like a tail, face twisted, shrieking. I ran for survival, heart thumping, legs moving automatically. Dove into the crib, yanking a blanket over myself.

She found me. Pressed the iron onto my bare arm. I screamed. Then I realized it was stone cold. She laughed. I lay there, shaking, stunned, humiliated. That was life on Moscow Street. Whiplash emotional shifts where joy and terror shared the same five minutes. Cold, chaos, fear. Survival. Somehow, I survived.

One night, Jun and I were fighting, each convinced the other had started it.

Mom never tolerated us fighting. Her voice cut through the chaos: "Stop it! Or else!"

But Jun had to push it further, finger wagging, smug grin, taunting, "Ha ha, you're in trouble!"

I argued back, tears welling, shouting it was his fault. My cries grew louder. Mom had no patience left. In one swift motion, she flung open the back door and shoved me into the backyard.

The cold air hit me like a frozen abyss. Pitch black. Teeth chattering, skin prickling. Monsters, murderers, or raccoons lurked just beyond the shadows. I was sure of it. I pounded on the door, shrieking until my voice turned raw. Minutes stretched out. Every shadow seemed alive. Finally, the door creaked open. Mom stood there, arms crossed, hair frazzled, more exasperated than concerned. I stepped inside, cheeks burning, heart racing. Jun grinned, thrilled with the chaos. I vowed revenge.

Then came the infamous Mom's Running Away Night. Another evening, all three of us were fighting and screaming, and Mom had finally had enough. Suitcase in hand, she threatened to leave forever unless we promised to behave. Emotional hostage situation. We cried, clung to her legs, begged her to stay. Of course, she didn't leave. She set down the suitcase, dusted off, and returned to her tasks.

Naturally, I tried the same move. Not long after, another loud fight with Jun broke out. Mom blamed me for all the noise. I got the scolding with her slipper. That was the last straw. I packed my little suitcase, heart hammering, convinced this was my moment. "I'm running away," I cried.

Mom barely glanced up. "Go ahead," she said. Jun even offered to tie my Fisher-Price Humpty Dumpty TV to the suitcase. No one tried to stop me. I marched down the steps, suitcase swinging, imagined a dramatic scene, then slowly turned back toward the house, carrying my suitcase full of rejection.

Moscow Street taught me fear and survival. Santa Rosa Avenue would teach me something colder: how it feels to be unwanted in your own home.

CHAPTER 3
FOUND IN A DUMPSTER

I didn't realize childhood could get darker. Santa Rosa Avenue proved it could, and almost immediately.

We moved into our house on Santa Rosa Avenue when I was eight years old, just up the block from Corpus Christi Catholic Church, a place that should have been a sanctuary, but for me, it was anything but. I wish I could say life became lighter, or that I finally found some peace there. But I'd be lying. If anything, the weight got heavier.

Every Sunday morning, like clockwork, Mom would storm through the hallway ordering us to get dressed for Mass. No excuses. No mercy. The girls were forced to wear veils, and if we couldn't find one, she'd yank a handkerchief from her purse and pin it onto our heads with bobby pins that stabbed our scalps. No one explained why. No questions asked.

Mass never made any sense to me. The priest spoke in riddles, or maybe it was just Latin; I couldn't tell. All I knew was that his tone always sounded like he was furious. Like we were all rotten sinners and he was there to remind us of it. I didn't walk out of that church with peace in my heart or any understanding of God's love. No. I walked out heavy. Guilt clung to me like a second skin.

That guilt followed me long after I left those pews. It became the quiet current beneath my life, the whisper behind every mistake and every failure. Whenever I messed up, or even when I didn't, Mom's words cut deep. I was bad. I was wrong. I was a disappointment.

I was ugly.

That wasn't just a feeling; I was told so by my siblings as well as my own mother.

She'd laugh at my awkwardness and pick apart how I looked, as if my appearance were a flaw to mock. So when kids at school joined in, I barely reacted. Why would I? My mother had already said it first.

One day there was a party at our house. A cute little girl and her mom were in attendance, and Mom was all smiles, fawning over the child's sweetness and joking that she'd replace me with her. It didn't feel like a joke to me. I grabbed the big wooden spoon that every Filipino kitchen seemed to have hanging on the wall and whacked the girl in the face. She bled, a small scratch, nothing serious, but I got in so much trouble my ears burned from Mom yelling at me.

One of the cruelest jokes, one that everyone seemed in on, was Jun telling me every so often that I'd been found in a dumpster and the family had taken me in out of pity. He said it casually, like it was a simple fact, as though he were stating my place in the world. And in a way, it almost made sense. I wasn't the beautiful one. I wasn't the boy. I wasn't the baby. I was awkward, unsure, always reaching for scraps of affection. They must have felt sorry for me, I thought. That's why I was here.

Every time Jun said it, Joji and Mom laughed along. It wasn't a one-time tease; it was a ritual. The joke always landed on me, and no one ever came to my defense. Not once. The silence became its own cruel proof.

One day, Jun wouldn't let it go. He hammered the story over and over, each word a tiny shove. I tried to argue, to insist it wasn't true, but my voice was thin and trembling, the voice of someone who wasn't sure anymore.

Finally, he disappeared into his bedroom, locking the door behind him. When he returned, he held a sheet of paper, a neatly typed "official" document, complete with signatures and stamps. It stated, in black and white, that I had indeed been found in a dumpster and adopted by the Guevara family.

I remember staring at the words, my whole body going still. The paper blurred as my eyes filled, but not before I read enough. My heart dropped into a pit so deep I could almost hear it echo. The blood drained from my face. In that instant, it hit me: he wasn't joking. All the laughter, all the silences, all the times no one stepped in, they were telling the truth.

I felt myself folding inward. My chest tightened until I could barely breathe. My eyes burned. I started crying harder than I'd ever cried in my life. Not the kind of crying that passes, but the kind that shakes your whole body and leaves you gasping. In that moment, I wasn't their daughter or their sister. I was a stray. A mistake. Something picked up off the street because nobody else wanted me.

Nobody loved me. They pitied me.

That was the story I told myself because it was the only one that made sense.

I didn't know what "depression" meant back then. I just knew the feeling of being invisible. Disposable. I was living inside it every single day, wearing a smile on the outside while sinking further into the dark on the inside.

From that moment on, I believed the story completely. No one ever said otherwise. No one tried to soften it or tell me I belonged, not even my own mother. She never stepped in to shield me or offer comfort. Instead, she seemed to hold Jun in a different light, like he was some kind of little king. Even at a young age, he was a great comedian, a natural leader, someone whose antics always earned her laughter and approval.

I watched her eyes light up when he was around, how she smiled at his jokes and excused his mischief. And there I was, silent, shrinking, invisible. It felt like I was nothing more than a shadow on the wall, hollowed out from the inside. Every laugh she gave him felt like a door closing on me, every glance his way a reminder that I was always just a little less.

That kind of love, or what passed for it, left me aching, feeling both unseen and unwanted, as if I was waiting for someone to say I mattered. But no one ever did.

Still, not everything in childhood was doom and gloom. There were fleeting moments, thin, shimmering slivers of joy. One of them was our annual trip to the Emporium department store on Market Street in San Francisco. Every Christmas, we'd sit on Santa's lap, ask for gifts we knew we'd never get, and pick a wrapped present from the big bin, each one a mystery. There were rides on the rooftop, too, spinning teacups and tiny trains that circled a painted winter wonderland. For a few hours, it felt like magic.

Until the year I got lost.

I must have been about six or seven. Mom was downstairs in the bargain basement, digging through sales racks like a woman on a mission, her focus razor-sharp. Joji had said she needed to use the bathroom, and without thinking, I suddenly decided to follow her. But somewhere between the racks of discounted sweaters and the endless rows of shoppers, I lost her.

I couldn't find the restroom. I doubled back to the register, heart hammering, scanning the crowd for Mom. I couldn't find her. Nothing. She was gone.

Panic hit me like a wave. My throat closed up, my legs turned to stone. All around me were strangers, loud voices, perfume, rustling coats, the harsh buzz of fluorescent lights overhead. The crowd felt like an ocean, and I was a small thing being dragged under.

I went up to the first woman I saw and told her, "I'm lost," my voice cracking like a whisper. She crouched down, said something soothing I couldn't even process, and next thing I knew, I was sitting behind a desk in a small office tucked away from the noise. The walls were beige, the air stale. Someone handed me crayons and paper and told me to draw while they located my family.

But I didn't draw.

I broke the crayons, one by one, snapping them clean in half. I shredded the paper into tiny pieces until my hands shook. I wanted to scream. I wanted to disappear. In that moment, I was sure no one was coming for me. That they hadn't even noticed I was gone.

Time stretched. Minutes felt like hours. The hum of the building was deafening. My heart kept beating against my ribs like it was trying to escape.

And then, finally, the door opened. A woman stepped in and told me they had found my family and that I should follow her. She led me out, and there they were—Mom, Joji, Jun, Jane in her stroller, and Dad. I froze when I saw him. Dad had left work to come find me. For a flicker of a moment, my heart lifted. Maybe, just maybe, I mattered enough for him to be here.

But then he looked over at Mom and said in Tagalog, "Ah, si Janette pala ang nawala? Akala ko si Joji." (Oh, it's Janette that got lost? I thought it was Joji.)

And just like that, the flicker went out.

He turned and walked away, back to work, leaving me standing there with the echo of his words. That's the part that stayed with me. Not the rescue, but the realization that even in the moment I thought I mattered most, I was still the afterthought.

And if home had already taught me I didn't matter, school was more than willing to make sure I never forgot it.

CHAPTER 4
PLAYGROUND POLITICS

Recess was supposed to be my favorite part of the day, twenty minutes of freedom. But one afternoon, I was in the bathroom, perched on a cold, hard toilet seat far too big for my small third-grade legs. The fluorescent lights hummed overhead, buzzing like trapped mosquitoes. Then I saw them. A pair of eyes peeking through the crack of the stall door. Not blinking. Just staring. Another pair appeared. Then another. One set. Two. Three.

Then the giggling began. Soft at first, a little tsk-tsk, then louder, sharper, echoing off the tile walls. Every rustle of paper, every shift of my shoes, fed their amusement. My chest tightened. My stomach knotted. I wanted to vanish.

When I finished, I waited, heart hammering, until the voices faded. Silence. I unlatched the door and froze. The mirror directly in front of me was plastered with sticky notes:

"CHICKEN LEGS."

"BUG EYES."

"CHECK OUT HER HUGE FRONT TEETH."

"GO AWAY, WEIRDO."

Something snapped inside me. I stepped forward, hands shaking as I grabbed the first note, ripping it off the mirror. Then another. And another. Fast. Hard. Each tearing sound swallowed a bit of their laughter. When the last note hit the tile floor, I stared into the mirror. Red-cheeked, trembling lips, glassy eyes fighting back tears.

Moments like that did not end in the bathroom. They followed me into every school day.

Every morning, I showed up with heavy books and an even heavier heart, bracing for whatever fresh hell the playground had in store for me. I was not popular. I was not pretty. I was skinny, bow-legged, and invisible in the way that makes you painfully aware of your own existence. Still, I showed up, hoping each day might be different. It never was.

There was a twisted little game we played at recess called "Who's the Prettiest?" A group of girls would form a circle, holding hands and skipping across the sun-beaten schoolyard. We would trap someone in the center like prey and sing in sugary, taunting voices:

"Who's the prettiest?"

The girl in the middle would scan our faces, then point to her pick. There was always someone. Just never me. Not once. My name did not even hover in the air. I could have vanished mid-game and no one would have noticed.

But when the chant flipped to "Who's the ugliest?" the circle tightened. Smiles sharpened. The air got heavy with the thrill of cruelty. And guess who they picked? Every. Damn. Time. *Me.*

I laughed along. That is what you do when you are the punchline. You laugh before anyone else can. You pretend it is fine so nobody sees the cut. But deep down, I got the message. I was not just failing some unspoken beauty test. I had become the living warning sign. Don't be like her. And in some twisted way, I agreed with them.

I probably would have been better off as a loner, head down, eyes forward, avoiding the crowd. But I could not help it. I wanted to belong. I needed to belong. So I did what I could. I lingered at the edges of conversations, laughed at jokes I did not even understand, tried to inch into cliques that had already closed their doors. I was not cool, but I was persistent. For someone so unpopular, I had a weird amount of confidence, or maybe it was just desperation in a clever disguise.

By fifth or sixth grade, I had my sights set on a group of girls who seemed just out of reach, cool enough to matter but not yet cruel enough to dismiss me completely. We were circling friendship, or at least something that looked like it. Then one day, during lunch or recess, one of them casually threw out a marvelous idea. By marvelous, I mean completely idiotic. They suggested I should call someone down.

It was not a dare. It was a test, an initiation. That was the term we used: calling someone down. It meant inviting another kid to fight you. A social gamble disguised as bravery. In the warped logic of grade-school politics, it also meant you were tough, or popular, or at the very least, not invisible.

I was not prepared. I was not even mad at anyone. But the idea of being accepted was louder than the voice in my head saying, *Are you insane?* So I nodded. Sure. Fine. If that was the price of belonging, I would pay it.

They even picked my opponent for me, Paulette Landers, a pretty girl who was popular, confident, and completely on board. The fight was scheduled for last recess the next day. I was not part of the planning. I just nodded along. I had no idea what I was doing. I had never been in a real fight, just scraps with siblings, most of which I lost. But suddenly, I was the undercard in a match I had not asked for.

When the final recess bell rang, the playground buzzed like a stadium. Word had gotten around. Kids whispered, pointed, waited. I walked out from one end of the yard with the girls behind me like a scrappy, clueless little contender being hyped by her "trainers." Paulette walked in from the other side like she had been training for this moment her whole life. We met in the middle. The crowd closed in.

Just as the first word might have been spoken, teachers swooped in and shut the whole thing down. No punches. No trash talk. Only a wave of disappointed boos from the audience and two confused girls being marched inside like criminals.

We were escorted to the principal's office to explain ourselves.

Paulette went first. "She called me down," she said, as if it made perfect sense.

Then it was my turn. "I don't know why. I didn't even want to," I mumbled. And that was the truth. I did not know why I agreed. All I knew was that I was tired, tired of standing alone, tired of being outside the circle. Somewhere in my little kid brain, I believed that maybe, just maybe, if I fought for a place, they would give it to me. Spoiler alert: they did not.

But even in a world that seemed determined to remind me I didn't belong, there were moments, unexpected and fleeting, that hinted at a different kind of magic waiting just beyond the chaos.

CHAPTER 5
CANDLESTICK MAGIC

Dad was a diehard San Francisco Giants fan. If he wasn't at Candlestick Park, he was in our living room, perched on the edge of the coffee table like a hawk watching its prey. He held a little transistor radio to one ear while the game blared on TV. He didn't trust the announcers to get it right. He needed both the radio guy and the TV guy, like he was trying to figure out the real story.

Baseball wasn't a pastime for him. It was a ritual. We, his kids, were background noise unless we were useful. Most of the time, that wasn't me.

Then one day, when I was eight years old, out of nowhere, he took me to a game.

Me. Not Jun. Not the favored son who usually got the golden ticket. That day, it was me. I still don't know why. Maybe Jun had homework. Maybe Dad was tired of him. Maybe the stars just lined up right.

He looked at me and said, "Get your jacket. We're going to the Stick."

Just like that, my heart nearly exploded.

I didn't ask questions. I didn't want to give him a reason to change his mind. I threw on my jacket so fast that one sleeve was inside out, and I bolted out the door. I was afraid if I blinked, it would vanish like a dream.

We took two buses to get to Candlestick Park. Two. The whole way, my excitement built like pressure in a soda can, ready to burst. I sat stiff and quiet beside him, stealing glances when I thought he wouldn't notice, trying to read his mood.

I don't remember if we spoke at all. Maybe we did. Maybe we didn't. I remember the hum of the bus, the city rolling by outside the window, my leg bouncing nonstop as if it had a mind of its own. I kept looking around, wondering if the other passengers knew where we were going, if they could feel the electricity running through me.

The ride felt endless and too fast all at once. Every stop brought us closer, and I held my breath, afraid the spell would break. But it didn't.

We were really going to the game.

And then we were there.

Candlestick was alive. It wasn't just a stadium. It was a beast made of concrete, steel, and sound. The air smelled of beer, popcorn, and something burnt. Peanut shells crunched under our feet. Fans in orange and black shouted as if their lives depended on it. Grown men painted their faces. Kids balanced sodas bigger than their heads.

And me? I was there. With my dad. At his church.

The thing is, I already knew the game. I had watched what felt like hundreds of Giants games on TV, sitting cross-legged on the carpet while Dad yelled at the screen. I knew how it worked with balls, strikes, double plays, squeeze bunts, all of it. I even knew the players' names: Tito Fuentes, Willie McCovey, Juan Marichal. They weren't just athletes to me; they were part of the soundtrack of my childhood I could pick out instantly.

But to see it all in person? The bright, perfect green of the field, the noise of the crowd, the sound of real cheers bouncing through the air, it was almost too much. Beautiful in a way I never expected. I felt like I had stepped inside the TV and everything had come alive.

We sat along the third-base line, close enough to see the sweat on the players' necks, close enough to feel the sharp crack of the bat deep in my chest. I silently prayed I would catch a foul ball.

I screamed my lungs out for Tito Fuentes, who had more swagger than anyone I had ever seen. I watched Willie McCovey step up to the plate like he owned the whole world. When he swung, it wasn't just a hit. It was a statement. The crowd roared, and I roared with them, hoarse, giddy, electric.

Somewhere between the hot dog and the seventh-inning stretch, sticky fingers, mustard on my cheek, heart thundering like a bass drum, I fell completely, irrevocably in love.

Not with Dad. With baseball.

For those nine innings, I wasn't the forgotten middle kid. I wasn't invisible. I wasn't a burden or an afterthought.

I was just a kid at the ballpark, lost in something bigger than pain, bigger than family. Part of the roar, part of the game, part of the magic.

And that was enough. That was the day my love for Giants baseball was born, but even on days filled with magic, I couldn't know that the world outside those moments could be cruel in ways I wasn't ready to understand.

CHAPTER 6
INNOCENCE INTERRUPTED

Our house sat seven or eight doors down from the church, where every Sunday after Mass people streamed past, familiar faces and casual chatter marking the rhythm of a neighborhood we thought we knew. That Sunday felt ordinary. Until it wasn't.

A tall young man, late teens, maybe early twenties, broke from the crowd and walked onto our porch. He asked if we had seen his cat. I said no. He pointed toward our neighbor Louisa's long yard, enclosed by a white fence, and asked if it might have gone in there. I said I didn't know. Then he asked if I would hop the fence with him to look.

I hesitated.

He said please a couple of times. Louisa was nearly a hundred and rarely came outside, so I didn't think she would mind. I glanced at Jane, still sitting on the steps, playing with her Barbie doll. I told her to stay, and she nodded. The young man jumped over first. I followed.

We wandered through Louisa's yard for a few quiet minutes. No cat. No real searching. I said I didn't think it was there and turned to climb back over the fence.

And that is when it happened.

I stepped up and attempted to swing my leg over the fence when I felt his hand, flat, steady, deliberate, pressed between my legs. It wasn't a push, stumble, or mistake. It was intentional. I dropped back down like I had touched fire. My chest tightened. The world tilted. For a split second, I couldn't tell if I had imagined it. Then I turned, and he was standing right behind me, calm, watching.

Then he exposed himself.

I didn't have a name for it. I just knew I hated it. Knew it wasn't meant to be shown. My stomach twisted. My heart raced, but my feet wouldn't move.

He asked if I knew what it was. I said no.

Then he asked if I wanted to touch it.

I couldn't speak. Couldn't scream. I just shook my head. Tears poured, fast and panicked, like they had been waiting beneath the surface. I wasn't just scared. I was ten, and Jane was four. We were outside our house on Santa Rosa Avenue, wearing matching pink ruffled dresses that Mom had a seamstress make for us during our recent trip to the Philippines. The front porch was our stage, our fortress, the place we felt safest from cars and strangers passing by.

I was sickened. I felt a kind of shame I couldn't understand, as if something had been taken from me without anything physical being stolen.

And just like that, he turned and jumped over the fence. His footsteps faded as he ran up Santa Rosa Avenue and disappeared around the corner, like it had been nothing at all.

There were other incidents during those years while living on Santa Rosa Avenue. My parents rented the downstairs to a married couple, Arnold and Schon. Schon was quiet and pretty. Arnold was loud and funny, his oversized jaw and big teeth making him look a little like Donald Duck. At first, nothing about them seemed unusual.

Schon was a nurse and sometimes worked evenings. On nights she was gone, Arnold would sometimes come upstairs to watch TV with me while Mom was busy cooking in the kitchen. It started small, with hands on my shoulders, massaging my neck and back, but he always stopped when Mom walked in.

I don't remember exactly when it escalated. One day, his hands slid lower, to the front of me, above my stomach. He rubbed my budding breasts and sometimes squeezed my tiny nipples. I froze. My chest tightened, my face burned, and a queasy shame rose in me that I couldn't name. Something felt wrong, dangerous, dirty. I said nothing. I sat still and silent, afraid to move, afraid to speak, afraid of what would happen if I did. Part of me thought I must have done something to invite it, and that thought was punishment in itself.

I don't know how long it lasted. Maybe the whole year they lived downstairs. Later, I understood clearly: a trusted adult crossed a line, leaving me sickened, frightened, and guilty for reasons I didn't understand.

I was eleven or twelve when it happened again. I was riding the 14 Mission bus, sitting toward the back on side seats that faced each other. An older man sat across from me. At first, I noticed his hand moving, his lap shifting, then his hands rubbing at something in a way that immediately made me uncomfortable. I turned away, trying to disappear into the bus window. When I looked back, he was holding something in his hand.

It was the same thing the young man from Louisa's yard had shown me a year or two before. His hand moved frantically. A moment later, there was a spray of something I didn't understand. I was the only other person on that side of the bus. My heart pounded. My skin prickled. I felt pinned, sick, and trapped, my mind trying to make sense of what I was seeing.

I didn't know what was happening. I only knew it was wrong and I needed to get away. Relief flooded me when the bus finally stopped. I got off as fast as I could, my stomach tight and legs shaky, telling myself again that it was best to keep it to myself.

Even on the safest porches, the world could reach in and take something from me I would never get back, teaching lessons I wasn't ready to understand.

CHAPTER 7
CHICKEN LEGS RUNS FOR PRESIDENT

In fourth grade, I did the unthinkable. I ran for class president. Four classrooms, about 125 students, and me—the most unpopular kid in the bunch, all big eyes, big teeth, and chicken legs. I had no chance, but something nudged me, maybe a hope that Mom would notice, maybe that I could make her proud.

There were only three students on the ballot, including me. When I told Mom, she actually showed interest. She seemed proud. I made flyers and handed them out in the schoolyard to anyone who would take one.

On election day, I nervously filled out my ballot and dropped it in the box, fingers crossed. The next day, we received the results. I wasn't shocked that I didn't win, but I was disappointed and terrified to face Mom. The winner was Brenda, the smartest, prettiest, most popular girl in the fourth grade. Second place went to Paula, who automatically became vice president.

I dreaded going home. As soon as I walked in the door, Mom was in the kitchen. "So, did you win?" she asked.

I lowered my head and whispered, "No, I lost."

She let out a short laugh that stung, so I immediately added, "By one vote."

The truth? I probably only got one vote, and that was my own. Mom softened her tone and said, "Oh, that's too bad." Later in life, I realized that laugh was her nervous way of handling words when she didn't know what to say.

A couple of months later, at a parent-teacher conference with Miss Caruso, Mom listened as my teacher praised me for always turning in assignments on time and being a great student. Then, out of nowhere, Mom said, "Yes, I know, and we were so disappointed when she didn't win president."

Miss Caruso nodded politely. "Yes, I was rooting for her."

Panic surged. I blurted out some random question just to change the subject. I was terrified Mom might say something about me losing by only one vote and discover that I hadn't. But she didn't. Mom never learned that I had not just lost. I had been crushed in a landslide. Keeping that secret felt like a small victory, a thin shield against the deeper humiliation I would have carried if she knew just how completely I had failed.

Even after the sting of losing, that tiny, stubborn spark inside me refused to die, carrying me forward into seventh grade and another moment that would test just how far I was willing to go to belong.

CHAPTER 8
NEWSPAPER POM POMS

I decided to try out for cheerleading in the seventh grade. Don't ask me why. Just like when I ran for class president in the fourth grade, it wasn't logical. It was madness. Something reckless would take over, a sudden surge of courage that pushed me into things I had no business attempting, like throwing myself into a fire just to see how bad the burn might be.

I wasn't popular. I wasn't even a blip on the radar. No friends. No social standing. Just a quiet, awkward shadow watching the popular girls from the sidelines. The ones with feathered hair, shiny lip gloss, and that effortless way of moving through the world like it already belonged to them.

Trying out for cheerleading wasn't just unrealistic. It was social suicide.

I had no training. I'd taken ballet and tap when I was younger, but those classes were more like glorified daycare. I was always off-rhythm, two steps behind, pretending to follow along when I had no idea what I was doing. I danced like my limbs belonged to different bodies.

Still, I showed up. Because why not add one more failure to the list?

The gym buzzed when I arrived. Girls stretched and chatted in small clusters, laughing with an easy confidence I'd never been able to fake. Most were trying out in pairs or little groups. No one stood alone. No one brought props. They wore cute dance outfits, shorts that fit just right, tank tops, and leg warmers. Meanwhile, I stood there in oversized white shorts that ballooned around my legs and a T-shirt that might as well have said *I don't belong here* in flashing neon.

And then there were the pom poms.

I had made them myself using strips of newspaper taped to sticks. I thought they were clever. I'd even been proud of them—until I realized no one else had brought any. Not one girl. No props. No gimmicks. Just skill. Just cool. Just them being everything I wasn't.

To make matters worse, I brought a 45 record with me that had Joji's old recital song from tap class, "Hey, Look Me Over" by Ronnie Hilton. A marching tune from another era. It felt like comfort food to me. But in that gym, surrounded by girls dancing to pop hits and funk tracks, it might as well have been elevator music at a morgue.

As I watched each audition, my stomach twisted tighter and tighter. One by one, the girls stepped up with polished routines set to modern songs, all crisp movements and confident smiles. They'd clearly prepared, choreographing every second. Their bodies moved like they belonged to the music. They were exactly what cheerleaders were supposed to be.

And me?

I sat in the corner clutching newspaper pom poms and a record from the wrong decade, slowly shrinking inside myself.

Then they called my name.

I didn't move.

My heart slammed so hard it rattled my vision. My hands went cold, fingers stiff around the sticks of my ridiculous pom poms. My name echoed again, louder this time. Every head turned. I stayed frozen, convinced that if I didn't move, maybe the moment would pass. Maybe they'd skip me.

They didn't.

Someone on the panel looked up from their clipboard, scanned the room, and locked eyes with me. The pause stretched. The room went quiet.

I couldn't breathe. My feet felt like cement as I walked toward the stage, each step thudding in my head like a war drum.

By the time I reached the floor, the silence was deafening. I handed over my record and watched them place it on the turntable like they were about to drop the needle on my public execution.

The record crackled. Then the music began.

I had no plan. No routine. No muscle memory.

Nothing.

Panic took over. I started marching in place, the way Joji used to during her recitals. I threw the top of my hand under my chin, copying her signature pose. Bits of her choreography surfaced as mismatched fragments that didn't belong together.

So I improvised.

I marched clumsily. I waved my arms. I swung the newspaper pom poms like I was flagging down a rescue helicopter. It felt like watching a mime have a seizure, and I knew it. I felt how wrong it was, how painfully out of place I looked.

The girls offstage giggled behind their hands, whispering and nudging each other. The adults tried to mask their reactions, but I saw it. Tight smiles. Eyes darting away. Polite horror.

And still the song marched on.

When it finally ended, I was drenched in humiliation. Sweat pooled behind my knees. My face burned. A few claps trickled out, maybe pity applause, maybe obligation. Or maybe I imagined them just to survive.

I walked off the stage like a condemned prisoner, head down, heart hollow. Another bruise no one could see. And still I wondered why I kept doing this to myself.

The answer didn't come. All I knew was that the results would be posted the next day outside the auditorium.

I already knew my name wouldn't be there. That wasn't pessimism. That was reality. I'd flailed around with newspaper pom poms and marched to a song no one under fifty recognized. There was no chance I'd made it.

So the next day, why did I find myself walking toward the auditorium?

Why was I letting my legs carry me down that hallway like I belonged there?

The list was taped to the wall near the stage doors, fluttering under a vent like it was mocking me. A single sheet of paper. Eight names.

The other girls crowded around it, calling names, hugging, squealing. I stayed back, heart pounding, hands clenched, waiting until the crowd thinned.

Then I stepped forward.

My eyes scanned from the top. Melissa. Tina. Valerie. Jessica.

Four.

I moved down. Nightingale. Rosanne. Arlene.

I stopped.

At the very bottom, as if added last—or written after a pause—was my name.

Janette.

I blinked. Read it again. Counted the names.

Eight.

And the last one was mine.

Shock came in waves. Not joy. Disbelief. Suspicion. I knew I hadn't earned it. No one could watch what I'd done and think, *Yes, that's cheerleader material.*

This wasn't a victory. It was mercy.

Maybe they felt sorry for me. Maybe they thought giving me one small win would help. Or maybe they just couldn't bring themselves to cut the sad girl with newspaper pom poms and baggy white shorts.

But pity or not, my name was there. I was in.

Nightingale was captain, loud and bold and a natural leader. Rosanne was soft-spoken and kind, her smile steady and warm. And Arlene—effortlessly beautiful, magnetic, her long black hair falling like it had never known a bad day.

And somehow, I was going to be standing next to them. Cheering beside them.

I didn't feel confident. I didn't feel like I belonged. What I felt was smaller and more fragile, a quiet loosening in my chest, like a door I'd been pushing against for years had finally given way.

It hadn't opened wide.

But it had cracked.

CHAPTER 9
UPWARDSTROKES

Whatever cracked open for me back then didn't transform me overnight, but it didn't close again, either. The confidence I had begun to gather in small, unexpected places slowly spread into other parts of my life. By the time I reached high school, I had started to make friends, not many, but enough. I wasn't popular, but I wasn't getting picked on anymore either.

I was beginning to grow out of my ugly duckling phase. Not that I had turned into anything remarkable. I wasn't a raving beauty, not by any stretch. My body was changing in ways that made me feel awkward and unfamiliar, hips and thighs growing heavier, breasts suddenly too large for my frame, leaving me unsure of how to carry myself.

I probably escaped much of the teasing anyway. I had enrolled in the school's work program, and as soon as I turned sixteen, my grades allowed me to take a very light class load. That meant most of my afternoons were spent at work, far from the scrutiny and petty cruelty of high school hallways. It gave me a small measure of freedom, a place to exist without the constant pressure of being seen and judged.

Around this time, the bullying at home finally stopped. Jane had never joined in, so she remained blameless. Jun left for the Navy soon after graduating. I remember the morning his ride came to take him to boot camp. It was still dark outside when I ran down the stairs to the garage to say goodbye. He kissed me on the cheek, surprising me, and as the car pulled away, a sharp twist settled in my chest. I realized, with a mix of pride and sadness, that I was going to miss my brother far more than I had expected.

Joji began taking more of an interest in me then. She invited me to join her for early morning workout classes at the community college, starting at

5:30 a.m. We would finish just in time for me to go home, freshen up, and head to school. She had taken modeling courses and started teaching me how to apply makeup properly.

"Never rub foundation into your skin," she told me. "Always use gentle upward strokes."

She showed me how to wear blush without looking like a clown and how to highlight the features that didn't embarrass me. I practiced what she taught, and I felt a quiet change. I could look at my reflection without immediately looking away. For a brief, shimmering moment, it felt as though the years of teasing and torment had loosened their grip. That small spark of confidence was electric, a feeling I had been starved for throughout my childhood.

By then, Mom's comments about my appearance had mostly faded, though she still slipped one in from time to time, more habit than cruelty. I'd grown a thicker skin, but the old sting lingered, a shadow I couldn't quite outrun. Dad remained distant. His swing shifts kept him away most days, and when he was home, his presence felt sharp and cold. He was strict with us, leaving little room for warmth or laughter.

And yet, in the quiet corners of my life, small pockets of light began to appear. Joji's attention, the early morning workouts, the careful lessons in makeup all stitched something new through old wounds. Slowly, I began to feel seen, not as a problem to be fixed or a disappointment to overcome, but as someone worth noticing.

CHAPTER 10
DEAR JOHN

The next chapter of my life arrived quietly, without warning, carried in on the footsteps of people I had never met but would never forget. It began with Joji, a new love in her life, and a change that would ripple into mine.

When Joji started dating Derek, a tall and slender Navy man, it was clear she had met someone special. Derek was incredibly smart, so much so that I nicknamed him the Walking Encyclopedia because he could answer almost every question on *Jeopardy!* without missing a beat. After dating for a while, they got married, and soon after, Derek's service took them to the East Coast. They lived there for a couple of years before moving back home to the Bay Area.

I was sixteen when Joji returned from the East Coast, and she did not come back alone. She brought Derek's entire family with her. His mother, three brothers, his sister, and her two little ones all followed her home to California. Derek's mother, whom we called Mom Cleo, was from the Philippines, and his late father was American, which made all of them mestizo. With their fair skin and striking features, you would never guess they had Filipino blood. To put it simply, they were a very good-looking family.

Joji and Derek stayed with us at first while searching for a place of their own, and as fate would have it, the rest of Derek's family found a house to rent directly across the street. Overnight, our quiet neighborhood turned into a lively extension of family with doors swinging open, voices calling out, lights on late into the night.

From the moment I met Mom Cleo, I was enchanted. She did not have to *try* to be impressive; she *was* impressive. She exuded quiet nobility, a presence that filled a room with elegance and mystery. I found myself wandering over to her house any chance I got, content to sit nearby as she lit a Pall Mall with perfect grace, elbow angled just right, exhaling like she had stepped out of an old Hollywood film. She told stories that sparkled with humor and heart, reminiscing about her youth or proudly bragging about her children. I could have listened to her for hours, and many times, I did.

And then there was Duane, the youngest of the brothers. He was eighteen years old, charming, confident, and too good looking for his own good. Joji warned me before he even arrived. She knew me well enough to predict that I would fall hard and quickly, but she also knew that Duane had not finished high school, and our parents, especially my dad, would never approve.

I tried to play it cool, but it was useless. Every time he talked, that East Coast accent made even ordinary words sound like something special. His smile, his laugh, everything gave me butterflies from across the room. What started as casual group conversations soon became stolen glances, stretching moments, and the kind of connection that made my heart race. Before I could even admit it out loud, I was in the middle of a full-on crush.

We were rarely alone. If Duane was around, his brothers or his mother were always nearby. But that never stopped me from popping over to see Mom Cleo under the guise of another long chat, only to end up lingering in the living room with the brothers afterward.

One night, the four of us, Duane, his brothers Dale and Tony, and me, decided to take Dad's massive Oldsmobile Delta 88 out for a joyride. My brilliant idea. Mom and Dad were out of town for the weekend, which in my sixteen-year-old mind meant freedom. Since I did not have my driver's license yet, Duane had the honor of driving. I directed them toward the hills not too far from our house, where we parked and admired the magnificent view of the city lights below. The air was warm, the music low, and for that brief moment, I felt so grown up, like we were on top of the world.

But the fun died the second we got home. That giant car suddenly felt too big for our tiny garage. Duane tried to guide it back in slowly. Then came the dreaded *screeeeech* from the passenger side. My stomach dropped. We froze. Another move forward or backward brought the same terrible screech. There was no escaping it. We all winced as he edged the car forward, metal grinding against the wall like nails on a chalkboard.

The damage was bad. The entire front passenger side had a long, ugly dent with the gold paint scraped away. My heart sank. There was no denying it; my parents would know the moment they saw the car. I barely slept that night, terrified Dad would notice immediately and kill me on the spot.

At sunrise, I called Duane. We walked eight blocks to the hardware store like two criminals on a mission and bought gold spray paint. It was not exact, but it was the closest match we could find. Back in the garage, he hammered at the dent and covered the scrape the best he could. It was not perfect. It was not even close. But it was the best we could do.

Miraculously, Dad did not notice. Not right away, anyway. Weeks later he casually mentioned that he thought Derek must have scratched the car while he was away. I kept my mouth shut. Derek unknowingly took the blame, and Dad never brought it up again. Sorry, Derek!

After the Oldsmobile incident, something evolved between Duane and me. We started talking more, every day if we could. Sometimes he would even come over to my house, which felt bold considering Dad's infamous scowl whenever boys were within a mile of me. Dad's suspicion only grew as Duane and I found more reasons to be together, but that did not stop the spark that was already burning.

One night, after Duane came over for a short visit, I remember having the worst toothache. But the moment he was there, laughing and talking with me, the pain faded into the background. All I could feel were the butterflies fluttering wildly in my stomach. When it was time for him to leave, I walked him out through the garage door, our usual path in and out of the house. We stood there for a moment, saying goodnight, neither of us eager to break the spell.

Then he leaned in and whispered, "I hope this makes your toothache better."

Before I could even react, he planted a soft kiss on my lips.

And that was it. I was in love. Or puppy love, I suppose, but I did not know that then. In my sixteen-year-old heart, it felt like the real thing. Duane became my first official boyfriend. Me at sixteen, him at eighteen. I felt pretty cool having an older boyfriend, like I had suddenly upgraded in life. Unfortunately, my parents did not share in the excitement.

It did not take long before Joji came into my room one night with a serious look on her face. She sat down and told me that Mom and Dad were not happy. They had sent her in as the messenger, and trust me, I got the message loud and clear. According to them, Duane was too old for me, he did not have a job, and worst of all, he had never graduated high school. In their eyes, that combination was a flashing red warning sign.

But I rebelled. For the first time in my life, this former ugly duckling did not feel so ugly anymore. Maybe I was finally growing out of that awkward phase or maybe love just had a way of making everything look better. Either way, I had a boyfriend. A real boyfriend. And not just any boyfriend, but a handsome one.

I strutted around with a confidence I had never known, proudly introducing him to my friends. I bragged about his age, how he was older and mysterious with that East Coast accent. I felt chosen. Special. Wanted.

So even with my parents disapproving and laying down their rules, I ignored every single one of them. Against their wishes, we were a couple, and I was not about to give that up for anything.

Duane was determined to win my parents' approval. He earned his GED, then landed a dishwasher job at the hospital where Mom worked. Ambitious and hardworking, he was always trying to do better. I encouraged him to apply at Wells Fargo Bank, where I worked in Personnel and often saw job openings. With persistence, he got hired in the same building as me, which felt exciting at first.

Though we worked in the same place, our paths rarely crossed since he worked the graveyard shift. Some mornings, as I arrived on the twelfth floor,

I would spot him from the window, leaving the building with coworkers. Then I started to notice a girl walking beside him. Just the two of them. Often. It became frequent enough to stir suspicion, though I stayed quiet at first, hoping I was wrong or maybe waiting for proof.

Eventually, jealousy got the best of me. When I confronted him, he seemed surprised, denying any involvement and claiming they were just friends. I wanted to believe him. After that talk, I never saw them together again, only him alone or with his usual buddies.

Months later, I was transferred to another department, ending my accidental window surveillance. One morning, as I crossed the back alley to work, I ran into a few of his coworkers. Their behavior instantly struck me as odd, jittery, avoiding eye contact, whispering to one another. One even turned back, as if signaling someone around the corner. My stomach dropped. Were they warning Duane?

Seconds later, Duane appeared, walking beside a girl. Not the same one from before. Someone new. He said something to her, and she slowed down, letting him approach me alone. He looked nervous, the guys looked guilty, and the girl just kept walking. No one said a word.

Something about the situation did not sit right. My intuition was screaming that something was off, and I began to suspect Duane was cheating. I did not say anything right away, but the unease never left me.

A few weeks later, I decided to skip work and surprise him. Since he lived right across the street, I waited until I saw him come home, then rushed over, grinning. He looked startled, maybe pleasantly so, I thought.

Not long after we went inside, the phone rang. Duane answered, but his eyes darted nervously side to side. My stomach tightened. He told the caller that Dawn, his sister, was not home and hung up quickly. The phone rang again, and this time his fidgeting was impossible to miss. Again, he told the caller Dawn was not home. My jealousy exploded. Without thinking, I grabbed the phone. Duane quickly muttered something into the receiver, hung up, and insisted it was just one of Dawn's talkative friends.

I did not believe him. Deep down, I knew. My instincts had always been sharp, and they were screaming the truth. Still, I pushed the thought away, telling myself the truth would surface eventually. I just wasn't ready to face it.

But I couldn't let it go. My need for answers took over, quiet at first, then relentless. Before long, I knew her name and how to find her. One evening, while Duane was at work and I was home visiting Mom Cleo, I finally gave in to the urge.

I went into his room and lifted the mattress. My heart dropped. Three Polaroid pictures of her, the same girl I had seen walking with him, stared back at me. In each one, she posed beside his black Z28 Camaro. My hands trembled as I turned them over, my breath shallow. Then I saw it—a card with a teddy bear holding a heart.

I froze, unable to look away. Every piece fell into place. My stomach twisted as disbelief and confirmation collided inside me. I had known in some part of my mind, but seeing it, holding it, made the truth undeniable. I had my answers, but the cost was a hollow ache that settled deep in my chest.

"Dear Duane," it read. "I love you. Love, Mary."

That was it. Proof. The cold stab of betrayal hit like ice water to my chest. My first real boyfriend, my first real heartbreak. He had shattered my young, naive heart, and I did not even know how to breathe, let alone know what to do next.

Without thinking, I bolted out of their house, ran across the street, and went straight up to my bedroom. My mind was spinning, my emotions a tangled mess of anger and heartbreak. Then, as if on autopilot, I reached for the slip of paper where I had written down her phone number.

Before I could even process what I was doing, I dialed. My hands trembled as I held the receiver to my ear. My heart pounded violently as the ringing filled the silence. After a few rings, a kind older man's voice answered.

"Hello," he said.

My own voice trembled so much that I barely recognized it as I asked to speak to Mary.

"She is not home right now," he replied gently. "Would you like to leave a message?"

I think I may have been sobbing when I asked when she might be back. There was a pause before he spoke again, his voice laced with concern.

"You sound upset. Are you okay?"

The kindness in his voice only made the lump in my throat grow. I swallowed hard, forcing myself to steady my breath.

"I am fine," I lied. "Thank you for your time."

And before I could fall apart any further, I quickly hung up the phone.

I locked myself in my room for the rest of the night, my mind racing with how I would even begin to confront Duane about this betrayal. When morning came, I was still so upset that I decided to call in sick to work. I had made up my mind. I would wait for Duane to come home from work, and then I would confront him.

I spent that morning sitting by my bedroom window, eyes fixed on Duane's house, waiting. Every sound made my heart jump, but then I heard it, the deep, throaty rumble of his Camaro climbing the hill. My stomach twisted as I saw him pull into the driveway. I did not even think. I bolted out the door, sprinting across the street toward him.

Just as I reached the edge of the driveway, a silver car turned in and stopped beside him. My heart dropped. It was her. Mary.

Duane got out of his Camaro, his face lighting up with a smile as he walked toward her car, until he saw me. Suddenly, everything changed. His face drained of color. The smile vanished. What replaced it was something between shock, guilt, and panic.

He tried to play it off, slamming the car door shut as if that could erase what I had just seen. But something inside me gave way. My body moved before my mind could catch up. I lunged forward, yanked her car door open, and reached in, ready to swing at her.

Before I could even land a hit, Duane grabbed me from behind, pulling me back hard. The door slammed shut with a bang.

"Drive away!" he barked at her.

Mary froze for a split second, her wide eyes meeting mine. I glared at her, every nerve in my body shaking with rage. *Say something*, I dared her silently. *Just one word.* But she said nothing. Instead, she turned her face away and sped off, the tires screeching as the silver car disappeared down the street.

Needless to say, that was it. I was done. I broke up with him right then and there. But Duane would not accept it. He showed up, called, begged, promising over and over that it was finished with her. A few days later, we were on the phone, still arguing about it. He swore he loved me, that he could not live without me. I did not believe him. My heart was too raw, too broken.

Then his voice changed, quiet, trembling. "Look out your window," he said.

Confused, I got up and looked across the street. There he was, standing at his own window, staring right at me. His hands were on the sill.

"If you break up with me," he said, "I will jump."

For a moment, everything stopped. I could not breathe. My heart pounded so hard I could hear it in my ears. He was serious. I could hear it in his voice. Panic surged through me. My legs felt weak, my hands shaking as I pressed them against the glass.

"Duane, do not do it. Please do not do it," I begged. My voice cracked as the fear rose inside me. The idea of watching him fall… I could not bear it.

I did not know what else to do. So I caved. I told him I would not break up with him. The words felt heavy in my mouth, but the moment I said them, he stepped back from the window.

I remember standing there long after we hung up, my body trembling, tears burning in my eyes. I was not sure if I had just saved his life or lost a piece of myself.

Duane and I were boyfriend and girlfriend for a total of nearly two years. I graduated from high school and began working full time. We were both still working at Wells Fargo Bank, but there were no more episodes of him cheating on me with other employees, at least none that I knew of. Then he quit his job and enlisted in the United States Army, wanting to make a better life for himself and maybe for our future, if we were to stay together.

However, several months later while he was deployed elsewhere, something happened. I started to change. He wrote me letters quite often, but I had started going out more with friends. I was eighteen then, building a life of my own, and I did not feel like that sixteen-year-old girl who had fallen headfirst into puppy love anymore.

It was not that I stopped caring. I just knew deep down that we had outgrown each other. Still, I knew breaking up with him would hurt him, and that made it harder. He was out there trying to build something solid for us while I was quietly preparing to end it.

So, in true cowardly fashion, I did the worst possible thing. I sent him a Dear John letter. One of those letters every soldier dreads receiving. Looking back, I can still feel the weight of it, the guilt, the sadness, and that tiny, shameful sigh of relief that came after dropping it in the mailbox. I had no idea what I was doing back then, except following a feeling I could not ignore. The girl who once thought she would die without him was finally learning how to live without him.

CHAPTER 11
KIDNAPPED AT HARRAHS

By the time I was twenty-three, I had learned a few lessons about love, heartbreak, and trusting my own instincts. Manny, my boyfriend at the time, had been a steady presence in my life for about a year, and I was finally starting to feel like I could build a life of my own. We had just moved into a house together with our friends, Ester and Armando, and what was supposed to be a quick weekend getaway in Reno with them would turn out to be nothing like I expected.

One crisp fall weekend in 1983, we packed up for the trip. The neon lights, ringing slots, and smoky casino floors promised the perfect escape. We checked into Harrah's, laughed over late-night drinks, and gambled just enough to feel daring without going broke.

By Sunday morning, we were tired but still riding the high from the night before. After breakfast, we all agreed on one last round at the tables and slots, then planned to meet in the Harrah's parking garage at 11:00 a.m. to head home.

I wandered off to play blackjack and, in a rare streak of luck, won three hundred dollars. In those days, that felt like a fortune. I stood at the elevator counting the bills like a game-show contestant, tiny purse in hand, still floating from the weekend and completely unaware of how quickly everything was about to change.

The elevator doors opened. A man and a woman stepped in with me. Nothing about them stood out. My head was still at the blackjack table, replaying my win, and I didn't feel anything off. Not yet.

But the moment I stepped out into the dim concrete garage, the air grew heavy.

The man and woman flanked me, forcing my arms to my sides as they steered me toward a stairwell before I even understood what was happening. The man pulled a gun from his jacket and pressed it into me, jabbing it sharply as we climbed two flights of stairs. At the top, they led me to a parked car, where another man was sitting calmly in the driver's seat. I refused to get in. That's when the man raised his arm and pistol-whipped me across the face. The metallic crack rang out like a gunshot. A burst of white light exploded behind my eyes, my knees buckled, and I collapsed into the back seat. Pain shot through my skull. My cheek burned. My breath stuttered. I thought I might pass out, but I didn't dare. Not here. Not now.

This couldn't be real, couldn't be happening. But it was.

There were three of them. The man with the gun slid in beside me. The woman jumped into the passenger seat. Another man waited behind the wheel, calm and ready, like he had been expecting me.

The doors slammed shut. The car lurched forward.

I saw the parking attendant ahead. For a split second, I wondered if I could scream or throw myself out of the car. I opened my mouth, but I didn't even get a breath out before cold steel pressed into my ribs.

I tried to speak, to cry out, but nothing came. My voice was gone. To this day I still have nightmares where I scream and no sound escapes.

The car reeked of marijuana and cheap booze. They smoked and laughed and passed around a case of Coors, treating the whole thing like a joyride. I sat frozen beside the man who hit me, my heart pounding so hard it shook my chest. They never spoke to me. Only around me. I was cargo. I was nothing.

Then I noticed he was holding my three hundred dollars and my purse. He opened it, took out my last fifty dollars, and snatched my ring and watch from me, all with casual ease while I sat bleeding, humiliated, and shaking.

We pulled into a run-down liquor store. The driver strolled inside, returned with more beer, and climbed back in laughing. The casualness of it made my skin crawl. I stared straight ahead, trying to disappear into the upholstery.

We drove for what seemed like hours. Eventually, the city faded. Trees replaced buildings. Fewer cars. No houses. No people. My throat tightened. I tried to speak, to beg for my life, but nothing came. I felt like I was underwater, drowning in panic.

The car turned onto a dirt road leading into a secluded park. It looked like the beginning of a horror movie, only I couldn't walk out of this one.

When the car finally stopped, the man in the back seat scooted close, practically on top of me. He held his pistol and pressed his face near mine. I could smell cigarette smoke, marijuana, and beer on his breath. Fear surged, and I choked, fighting the urge to throw up. Then he moved the gun, tracing it down my thighs to my knees.

Oh dear God, I silently prayed, *please stop him.* But he didn't. He traced the gun up my arms, around my neck, and along the outline of my face, laughing and breathing heavily in my face. I felt like I was going to die right there.

Then the driver said, "Hey man, we gotta jet."

He gave me a big, sloppy lick across my face, jumped out of the car, stormed to my door, yanked it open, and hissed, "Get out of the car, bitch."

He grabbed my arm and ripped me out. I hit the ground hard, knees scraping across gravel, palms tearing open. Before I could even breathe, the girl from the front seat approached, grinning.

"I've always wanted to do this to someone," she said.

She slapped me. The sound came first, louder than it should have been, like a crack in the air. Then the pain followed, delayed, blooming across my cheek. The second slap felt distant, as if it landed on someone standing beside me. My ears filled with a high ringing, the kind that makes the whole world feel underwater.

She grabbed my hair. I felt the pull before I felt the pain, a strange tugging at my scalp, and then the burn, sharp and hot. Something tore. I wasn't sure if it was my hair or me. She spit in my face. I watched it more than I felt it, a warm streak sliding down my skin. I tried to move, to speak, but my body wouldn't respond. I was floating somewhere above myself, looking down at a girl frozen in place.

"That's enough," the man snapped. "We need to go."

She shrugged, laughing. "Just having a little fun." She walked back to the car, shaking her hand and muttering, "Ow, that really hurt."

I lay in the dirt, bruised and shaking, while their white Mustang screeched away, spitting dust into my face. The silence afterward was deafening. I had never felt more alone or disposable.

Everything was gone. My purse. My jewelry. My sense of safety. My legs trembled beneath me in my short black T-shirt dress and espadrilles. Far in the distance, I saw downtown Reno shimmering like a mirage.

Somehow I managed to get up. I started walking. Then I started running.

I didn't dare flag down a car. I didn't trust anyone. All I could think was get to Harrah's and find Manny.

The sun beat down as my feet pounded the pavement. Every step sent pain shooting through my body, but I kept going. I had run plenty of 10K charity races and knew how to pace myself, but this wasn't a race. This was pure survival.

When I finally reached the casino, Harrah's glowed like a beacon. I sprinted through the crowded floor, adrenaline carrying me toward the elevators that led to the parking garage, when I heard my name.

"Janette!"

It was Armando.

Everything inside me froze. Shame washed over me, heavy and hot. I darted into a restroom, slammed a stall door shut, and threw up. Fear and shock poured out of me all at once.

Ester's voice called my name. When I opened the stall, she took one look at my swollen eye, bleeding forehead, scraped knees, and trembling body, and wrapped her arms around me. We both cried, collapsing into each other. She guided me to the sink and gently cleaned the blood from my forehead and knees with cold, damp paper towels. Even her soft touch made me flinch. She kept asking what happened, and at first I couldn't speak.

Finally, in a hoarse whisper, I got the words out. "They took me. They beat me. I thought I was going to die."

Her face went pale. She held my hand as I tried to steady my breathing.

When we stepped out of the restroom, Manny and Armando were standing nearby. Their faces drained of color. Manny's panic turned quickly to anger.

"What happened? Who did this?" Manny demanded.

Ester held me tightly, her voice firm but trembling as she repeated what I had told her.

Manny's fists clenched at his sides, then he punched the wall hard enough to echo down the corridor.

A security guard happened to be in the area. Manny explained what had happened and insisted we needed the police. The guard nodded, radioed it in, and led us through a maze of back hallways into a windowless office. I was brought inside immediately, just me, and asked to explain everything that had happened. I wasn't sure who was questioning me, perhaps a manager from Harrah's, but he listened intently as I recounted the ordeal.

It didn't take long before two uniformed Reno police officers arrived. Shortly after, two plainclothes men walked in.

"We're with the FBI," one of them said as he opened his badge in front of me.

"FBI?" I repeated, the word catching in my throat.

"This is a federal case now. You were kidnapped."

The word hit harder than any slap.

Then two more men entered the office. They didn't identify themselves, but suddenly I realized I was surrounded by seven men, all firing questions at me at once—rapid, overlapping demands for descriptions, car details, license plates, voices, anything I could give them.

A wave of dizziness hit me so hard I could barely stay upright. Every word I managed felt like it was being picked apart, wrong before it even left my mouth. The room spun, voices overlapping, questions firing faster than I could process. I could barely string a sentence together. There was no counselor, no woman officer, no soft voice telling me it was okay. Just cold lights and relentless pressure. I couldn't shake the feeling that no one believed me, that I was the one on trial, the criminal under the microscope.

Later, a police officer took me back to retrace the route. Somehow, I don't know how, but I managed to spot the liquor store first, a small, familiar landmark in the haze of memory. Then I saw the dirt road that led up to the secluded area where they had thrown me out, and I pointed to the exact spot. Behind us, a dark vehicle slid to a stop. The FBI agents stepped out, moving with methodical precision, eyes scanning the ground, taking in every detail, every print, like bloodhounds on a scent. Each step they took made the world feel sharper, colder, more urgent.

Even then, I could not shake the feeling that I was somehow the criminal here, that the story I told, my terror, my pain, was not real to anyone else. My words felt small and fragile, barely holding together. I wanted to disappear, to fold into myself and erase the chaos that had ripped through my life.

Then one of the agents spoke. "Mustang."

The word hit the air like a spark. Proof.

My heart thumped. Someone finally believed me. The grooves in the earth matched the nightmare that had left me in the dust.

Back at the Reno Police Station, they told me I needed to meet with a sketch artist. Manny was allowed to sit with me.

The artist was impatient and sharp-tongued. Together we recreated the man who hit me, then the woman, whose face was burned into my memory. When it came to the driver, I barely remembered him. The artist pressed and pushed until I finally gave up and agreed to a sketch that looked nothing like the man. I just wanted it to be over.

Hours passed. By the time we left, it was dark. Harrah's never offered a room, a meal, or even a phone call. Nothing. We had bought McDonald's for the ride home, but I couldn't eat. I curled up in the back seat and fell asleep before we even hit the freeway, the motion of the car the only thing keeping me from falling apart completely.

The next morning my body screamed. My eye was swollen shut, my head pounded, and my limbs were bruised. I didn't see a doctor. I didn't talk to a therapist. I didn't ask for help. I iced my face, cried in the shower, and tried to pretend nothing had happened.

But something had happened.

Something that clung to me even in daylight.

I kept reliving the moment when my captor traced his gun across my body, the cold metal sliding over my skin, the terror rooting itself so deeply that it followed me into every quiet moment afterward.

Something that never left me.

And fifteen years later, it would happen again.

Another parking lot.

Another car.

Another nightmare.

Only that time it would be even worse.

CHAPTER 12
MANNY

After the chaos in Reno, Manny and I returned home forever changed. The weekend had been meant as a carefree escape, but it turned into something far more intense. Through it all, I realized how steadily he had been by my side, and how much I had come to rely on his calm presence. It was the beginning of a deeper connection that would shape the years to come.

I had met Manny through Joji's best friend, Myrna. She and I spent many nights at Studio West, a popular disco club that felt like the center of the universe in those days. We danced until our legs ached and sometimes stayed until the sun washed the night off our faces. One evening, she mentioned that her boyfriend was bringing a friend because they hoped to set us up. I shrugged it off, not expecting much.

When Manny and I were introduced, he asked me to dance, but I declined because I did not care for the song that was playing. The moment the music switched, another guy reached me before Manny could try again, and I said yes simply because I loved the beat. While dancing, I glanced toward Manny and saw something unexpectedly tender in his eyes. He looked disappointed, and guilt tugged at me. When the next song began, I walked straight over and asked him to dance.

The second we stepped onto the floor, everything changed. Manny moved with a smoothness I had never seen in a partner. He had an ease and elegance that made dancing feel effortless. Later I learned he had been a professional dancer on a popular television dance show in the Philippines, which made perfect sense. He moved like someone who had lived his whole life in rhythm.

Manny had only recently moved to the United States, but after that night he began going to Studio West as often as Myrna and I did. Before long, we started spending time together outside the club, and our connection deepened slowly, steadily. Over time, we became a solid couple.

He came from a big, traditional Filipino family, the youngest of six children. With all his siblings having kids, there were plenty of nieces and nephews, and the family was very close-knit. Everyone respected one another, and when they welcomed me and my family, it felt genuine and warm. My own family returned the sentiment, and I began to notice how much this sense of family connected me to both sides.

It was around this time, as Manny and I were growing closer, that I started feeling a deeper connection to Mom and Dad as well. They were thrilled that Manny came from a prominent family in the Philippines, especially Mom. Manny's father was the former president of a huge, well-known bank, and Mom was endlessly impressed by that kind of status. Their excitement made me feel proud and more connected to them, and soon I found myself spending more time at their home, soaking in the warmth and familiarity of family life.

Manny and I married soon after, and the following year we welcomed our first child, Kristin Joy Villatuya. Holding her in my arms for the first time filled me with awe and wonder. She brought a new depth of love, purpose, and joy into my life. Her laughter and curiosity became a daily reminder of the beauty and promise that life could hold.

Even as our family life blossomed, I began thinking about my own path. Watching Manny navigate his world with confidence, seeing Kristin grow and change every day, and feeling the quiet support of my parents reminded me that I wanted a life that was fully mine. The routines of family were comforting, but I felt the stirrings of curiosity and ambition, a quiet urge to explore something new beyond the walls of home and family.

CHAPTER 13
LEAVING CORPORATE LIFE

When Kristin turned one, I started browsing the classifieds for a new direction. I had been laid off from Wells Fargo after seven years, and though I had been pregnant with Kristin at the time, the news did not devastate me. In many ways, it felt like a relief. I had learned the systems, climbed the ladder, and played the part, but the structure and formality of the corporate world had never truly fit who I was. Stepping away gave me space to breathe again and to imagine something different for myself.

What I did enjoy in HR was interviewing people. Not the formal questions or the technical requirements, but the conversations. I loved asking about their backgrounds and listening to their stories. I found myself rooting for people, wanting them to find the right place even if it wasn't this job. That part of the work always energized me.

As I flipped through the classifieds, the staffing agency ads kept catching my eye. The idea of meeting different clients and interviewing candidates felt more flexible and more human, something that fit me in a way corporate life never had. Soon I found an agency called Office Mates 5 and went in for an interview. Their small, buzzing office was the opposite of Wells Fargo: phones ringing, people moving fast, and an energy that felt alive.

The interview was informal. They cared less about credentials and more about whether I could connect with people and handle pressure. I talked about my HR experience and how much I enjoyed interviewing.

Near the end, the woman interviewing me suddenly asked, "What's your zodiac sign?"

I laughed and said, "Taurus."

She nodded as if that explained everything and hired me on the spot.

The pay structure was another story. It was not a steady salary. I would be working on commission with the possibility of bonuses, and I would receive a small monthly advance that acted as a draw against future earnings. It was risky, especially with a young child at home, but something in me knew I needed to take the chance. It felt like the first step toward a life that was mine.

The learning curve was steep. Each day introduced me to new industries, job titles I had never heard of, and personalities that came at me faster than I could write notes. I had to move quickly, juggle clients and candidates, and trust my instincts. It was challenging, unpredictable, and sometimes overwhelming, but never boring. And best of all, I got to meet people, hear their stories, and help them find where they belonged.

CHAPTER 14
FINDING RHYTHM AND FRIENDSHIP

The first month was discouraging. I made two placements, which felt like a win, but the commission only covered my advance. After all that effort, my paycheck was zero. I remember staring at the numbers, wondering if I had made a terrible mistake.

But I kept going. I listened more closely, learned from each near miss, and slowly found my rhythm. Clients started calling back. Candidates remembered me. Each month inched forward, then jumped. I could feel myself improving, reading situations more clearly, and trusting my instincts more confidently.

Around that time, I grew close with one of my co-workers, Katie. We hit it off right away. There was something easy about our friendship. We often had lunch together, sharing stories and frustrations, celebrating little wins, and trading tips. She became one of the bright spots in my day.

Then, in my sixth month at the agency, Katie pulled me aside. She told me she had accepted a position with another staffing firm. They were planning to open a new division focused entirely on temporary job placements, as opposed to the permanent ones we had been working on. The owner of the new agency was looking for two people to launch the project, and Katie had recommended me.

The idea lit something in me. The thought of helping build something from the ground up was exciting. I did not hesitate. I jumped at the opportunity. It felt like a fresh start within a fresh start, and I was ready to be part of something new, something that could really grow.

Katie and I were given a huge office to share, just the two of us, and we worked incredibly well together. We had an easy rapport and a rhythm that made the workday move quickly. We divided tasks naturally, supported each other through slow days, and celebrated every small win. It helped that we genuinely liked each other, and we both believed in what we were building.

Our job was not limited to phone calls. One of the more surprising parts of our training involved something much bolder: physically walking into office buildings to solicit new clients. It was called "cold walking," and it was exactly what it sounded like. Unannounced, face-to-face introductions with office managers, receptionists, or whoever happened to be at the front desk. We brought brochures, business cards, and our most professional smiles, ready to make our pitch.

One day, it was just me and my boss, Cathy, doing the rounds. Cathy was a force. She was feisty, confident, and absolutely fearless. She was the kind of woman who did not wait for doors to open. She kicked them open herself. That day, we were canvassing an office building in the financial district, floor by floor, visiting every business we could. We must have gone through more than half a dozen floors, popping in, introducing our new service providing temporary help, and handing out materials like we belonged there.

We were on a roll, but when the elevator doors opened to the next floor, we were met by a surprise: a very large security guard standing squarely in front of us. My stomach flipped. He was tall, in full uniform, arms crossed, a clear signal that we were done. There was a brief pause as the air tightened.

Before he could speak, Cathy gave him a quick wave and said calmly, "We're going, we're going." She did not flinch. No apology, no explanation, just a confident exit. I was half nervous, half thrilled. The moment felt straight out of a movie. And judging by Cathy's reaction, I had a feeling this was not her first elevator standoff. Her boldness left a mark on me. I realized that confidence is not always about having a perfect plan. Sometimes it is about being willing to push boundaries, take risks, and walk into the unknown like you belong there.

With each experience like that, my own confidence grew, not in leaps, but in steady steps.

When we got back to the office, I could not wait to tell Katie what had happened. The second I launched into the story, she let out a snort, which of course set me off. Within seconds we were doubled over, crying from laughing so hard. It was lunchtime, so we did what we always did. We boiled water in our little hot water maker, tore open two packs of instant ramen, and called it gourmet. We practically lived on those soups back then. Money was tight and neither of us was earning much yet, but somehow we always managed to turn our broke-girl lunches into comedy hour.

We even kept a can of air freshener handy to keep the smell of our meals from drifting into the lobby. It became a running joke between us. Ramen, air spray, hustle, repeat. Those early days were not glamorous, but they were real. And somehow, through the struggle and the laughter, they were also some of the most fun I ever had at work.

CHAPTER 15
RUNWAY TO FIDM

Katie and I were already close, but we had become even more connected, the kind of work partners who carried each other through long days and tougher moments. So when she asked me to be a bridesmaid in her wedding, I was flattered. Manny and I drove to Oregon, and suddenly I was surrounded by her college friends, these beautifully bonded women with years of stories, inside jokes, and photo albums full of proof. I didn't have that. No sorority years, no college roommates, just my own patchwork of friendships. Watching them made me happy for her and a little wistful for myself, but mostly I felt honored that she wanted me there.

Back at work, I barely had time to settle in before Katie pulled me aside one morning and told me she was giving her notice. Her new husband had accepted a job in Southern California, and they would be relocating soon. I was devastated. Katie had made the job fun and manageable, and without her, I admitted it would not be the same. The work still leaned too corporate, and I never fully felt I belonged. Then Katie mentioned a job opening at a private fashion college that a friend of a friend had told her about. The word fashion made me sit up straight. Creativity, expression, and artistry called to me. It was a world I had to explore.

As soon as Katie mentioned the job opening at a fashion college, I wanted to know everything. The name alone lit me up. FIDM, The Fashion Institute of Design and Merchandising. It sounded like the kind of place I had only read about in magazines. And this was 1986, long before Google, online reviews, or websites. If you wanted information, you had to get out there and find it yourself.

So I decided to do exactly what I had been trained to do: a cold walk-in. I thought of Cathy, our boss, and smiled. She would be proud.

FIDM's San Francisco campus was located in a corner building at Market and Stockton Street, right by Union Square, the epicenter of the city's shopping district. *Perfect*, I thought. I walked in, took the elevator to the third floor, and stepped into the bright, modern lobby. The receptionist looked up as I approached.

"Hello," I said politely. "I'd like to see Kim Robinson, please."

Katie had told me to ask for her since she was the friend of a friend who supposedly had the inside scoop. I mentioned the referral, hoping it would give me a little credibility.

"Do you have an appointment?" the receptionist asked.

I admitted I didn't. She informed me that Kim was currently in an interview with a student and wouldn't be available for a while. Then she asked what the visit was regarding.

"I was referred by someone who knows Kim Robinson regarding the opening for an admissions advisor position," I told her. "I just wanted to get more information and was told she would be the right person to speak with." I added, "I don't mind waiting, and in the meantime, may I take a look at a college catalog?"

She hesitated, then nodded and said someone would bring one out shortly.

Several minutes passed before a stern-looking woman appeared. "I'm Gloria," she said flatly, clearly irritated at having been pulled from whatever she was doing. She handed me a catalog without much warmth, and I thanked her as genuinely as I could.

I dove into the booklet, flipping through every page, fascinated by what I saw. Programs in fashion design, merchandising, visual communications, it was all speaking my language. I was completely engrossed when Gloria returned, surprising me.

"The director has a few minutes to meet with you," she said curtly.

What? I couldn't believe it. I had only come in hoping to learn a little more about the job, maybe connect with someone who worked there. Now I was about to meet the actual director? My heart started pounding.

Gloria led me towards the glass-walled office. She knocked once, then opened the door and ushered me in.

The office was stunning, spacious, with huge windows that overlooked the lobby. And there she was, the director of admissions. She was absolutely striking as she rose from her desk in a white colored Adrienne Vittadini sweater and perfectly tailored trousers, exuding sophistication and command. She might as well have stepped out of the pages of *Vogue*. I extended my hand, doing my best to stay composed.

As she shook it, she said, "I don't normally meet with anyone without an appointment, but I have a few minutes."

I nearly had to pinch myself. I felt like I was meeting the editor-in-chief of a fashion magazine, not the director of admissions. But here I was, completely unplanned, utterly in awe, and absolutely determined to make the most of those few minutes.

I already knew I wanted the job before I even heard the details. Just being in that space, the energy, the atmosphere, the style, spoke to something deep inside me that had been waiting for a place like this. As she explained the role of admissions advisor, I clung to every word, eager to absorb it all. But even while I listened, I kept catching glimpses of the people passing by her office windows. Those wide panes of glass offered a perfect view into the heartbeat of the campus. Everyone walking by was fashionably dressed, effortlessly stylish. No stiff suits, no corporate uniforms. This was a different world. A creative world. And it felt like home.

The role itself excited me even more. I would be guiding students as they explored their dreams, helping them discover the major that truly fit them, and ultimately enrolling those who were ready to step into their futures.

As the director spoke, something clicked in me. This was what I had unknowingly been preparing for. I had spent the last five years interviewing candidates and matching them with job openings. I knew how to connect with people, how to ask the right questions, how to help them discover their potential even if they could not quite see it themselves. The only difference now was that instead of jobs, I would be guiding students toward an education built around creativity and toward careers in the fashion industry.

And that was the magic word: fashion.

This was not just a job. It was a purpose. It was the place I had imagined years ago when I first dreamed of working in an environment that inspired me.

Although I was doing my best to stay composed, I became hyper-aware of my outfit. I had carefully chosen it that morning because I thought it was fashionable and appropriate, but now, sitting across from this stunning, intelligent woman in her pristine white Adrienne Vittadini ensemble, I started to second-guess myself. Was I stylish enough? Did I belong here?

For a brief moment, the old insecurities crept in, but I pushed them aside. I wanted this job so badly there was no space for self-doubt. I focused on projecting passion, confidence, and genuine enthusiasm for the opportunity. I leaned into what I did have: my experience, my curiosity, my drive.

What was supposed to be a few minutes with me turned into an hour and a full-blown interview. I rose with her at the end, met her eyes, and shook her hand firmly. "Thank you for your time," I said, meaning every word. I also told her that I was very interested in the position and believed I would be a perfect fit for the job.

As I walked out of the building and onto the busy San Francisco sidewalk, my heart was racing. I felt like I had just stepped off a rollercoaster, energized, breathless, and full of hope. I was riding the high of possibility.

Then a sudden thought hit me: What if they don't call? What if I am not what they are looking for?

I pushed it aside immediately. I could not allow myself to spiral. I wanted this job too much to entertain doubt. I raced home, practically willing the phone to ring.

It was still early afternoon when I arrived home. If they were evaluating my interest, and if I had impressed the director, surely they would call before the day was over, right? But by 6:30 p.m., I convinced myself that they would not call that soon. Maybe they did not want to seem too eager. Yet I felt it in my bones that I was going to get the job.

The phone rang at 7:00 p.m. I picked it up without overthinking the late hour. It was Gloria. I was stunned for a moment, then remembered the admissions staff often worked later hours to better accommodate students. Suddenly, the timing made perfect sense. She asked if I could come in the next day to meet with the director of the San Francisco campus. Of course I agreed.

The next day, I arrived twenty minutes early. I wanted to be prepared and composed. The campus director came out to greet me and led me into her office, a bright, spacious room lined with large windows. She was a whirlwind, radiating excitement, speaking quickly, and overflowing with energy. When our meeting ended, she told me they hoped to hire as soon as possible and that I would hear back within the week. Then she called Gloria to show me around the admissions area and give me a feel for the environment. Gloria introduced me to several advisors, each of whom greeted me warmly. Everyone seemed genuinely happy to be there, which only confirmed what I already felt. This was where I wanted to build a career. This was where I wanted to grow.

The admissions advisors worked in private cubicles, about a dozen in all. Each space was personalized with photos, fashion sketches, colorful swatches, and little touches that reflected the individuality of the advisor who worked there. As I walked through, I could feel the energy of the place, the buzz of conversation, the creativity on the walls, the sense of purpose in the air. I wanted to belong there more than anything.

Then she led me down the hallway past both directors' offices. I peeked in and saw each of them deep in conversation with a student and their parents. It was a full-circle moment. Just the day before, I had been on the other side of that glass.

I thanked Gloria for showing me around, got in the elevator, and was flying high, full of excitement. Then, as soon as I stepped outside the campus, I thought, *Within the week?* After hearing from them just hours after my cold walk-in, a week suddenly felt like an eternity. But I kept myself in check. I had made it this far. I had made an impression. As I left the building, one thought stayed with me, strong and steady:

I belong here.

Two days later, I got the call. I was hired and would be starting in two weeks. I couldn't believe it, but then of course I did. This was a perfect fit.

When I arrived at the campus on my first day, I waited by the elevator, clutching my tote and silently rehearsing how to introduce myself. Then, like a scene out of a movie, the front doors opened, and the director of admissions walked in, as stunning and composed as ever. She smiled and made her way toward me, accompanied by another woman.

"This is Janette, our newest admissions advisor," she said warmly, turning to her companion. "Janette, this is Vivien from our Los Angeles campus, our vice president of admissions."

Vivien. The name alone felt regal, and the woman matched it. She looked like she had stepped right out of an episode of *Dynasty*, all sharp angles and elegance, draped in designer fabric, glittering in just the right places. Her hair, her posture, her confidence. It was intoxicating.

I smiled and shook her hand, but in that moment, I became acutely aware of one very inconvenient and embarrassing detail: my shoes. I was wearing a pair of old Reeboks, white, chunky, and ugly, my commute shoes. We didn't have stylish sneakers back then like we do now. My polished dress shoes were tucked away in my tote bag, waiting for their grand entrance. I glanced down, mortified.

In the corporate world, it was normal, expected even, to wear sneakers for the commute and switch into heels or dress shoes once you arrived. It was part of the unspoken rhythm of office life, especially for women who walked city streets and rode public transit. I had done it for years without a second thought. But this wasn't the stiff, cubicle-lined world of banking anymore. This was FIDM, where image and presentation were part of the culture, not just the dress code.

I wanted to disappear into the elevator and race to the restroom to change. Instead, I stood there in my sneakers, feeling wildly underdressed next to these two stylish women, and realized I had just been handed my first true lesson in fashion industry professionalism. I smiled, pretending I wasn't dying inside, and made a mental note to purchase a stylish pair of flats for the commute. This was the beginning of something entirely new, and ready or not, I was stepping into it.

That first day, I met the rest of the admissions team, about a dozen of us. We came from different backgrounds, but we shared a mission: to guide, support, and inspire. Weekly meetings covered strategy and curriculum changes. FIDM was an accredited college, so it wasn't just fashion and design—it was academics too. I had to learn it all. I had to listen in a way I never had before, to the dreams, fears, and doubts of students and their parents. They looked to me not just for information, but for guidance and belief. I studied every major, explained financial aid clearly, evaluated portfolios, read essays, and interpreted transcripts. The knowledge was intense, but I welcomed it. This wasn't corporate. It wasn't about climbing a ladder or collecting a paycheck. This was about impact.

A month of training passed in a blur of note-taking, shadowing, and practice. Then one morning, they told me I was ready. My first interview would be with a high school senior curious about interior design, the one major I knew least about. Determined not to blow it, I crammed the curriculum guide for days, learning about drafting, codes, regulations, and even math.

The day of the interview, he arrived with his parents and older brother. I greeted them warmly, hiding my nerves, and began by asking about hobbies and schoolwork. Then came the dreaded moment: the curriculum. I recited every class description from memory, sounding like a human brochure. From the corner of my eye, I saw the older brother slumped in his chair, fast asleep.

That was it. I had blown it. I could see the family's enthusiasm slipping as I droned on about "Environmental Lighting and Drafting Principles." I hadn't inspired them. I had bored them. Worse, I may have single-handedly dissuaded this young man from pursuing a career in interior design.

I learned a lot from that first interview. It humbled me. Memorizing and repeating straight from the catalog, no matter how well-rehearsed, wouldn't inspire anyone. Students weren't looking for a sales pitch; they wanted someone who could help them see themselves in this world. I began rewriting how I spoke about each major, putting the curriculum into my own words, using examples, storytelling, and heart. I wanted every student to feel seen, understood, and excited.

I became a sponge. I dove into everything I could find about the fashion industry, from designers and markets to trends, textiles, and manufacturing. I read fashion magazines cover to cover, including *Apparel News* and *Women's Wear Daily*, as well as anything else related to the industry. I watched documentaries, studied our faculty, and asked endless questions. I wanted to speak fluently in this new language. Eventually, I did. I became fluent in fashion, not just in vocabulary, but in passion and understanding.

Something amazing happened. I started enrolling students regularly, confidently, and joyfully. I found my rhythm. I found my place.

A couple of years in, our campus moved just up the block to 55 Stockton Street, right in the heart of Union Square. Now we were truly surrounded by fashion. Neiman Marcus stood across the street; Macy's on the other side. Chanel, Saks Fifth Avenue, and Louis Vuitton were just steps from our front door. It was electric. This wasn't just a job anymore; it felt like I had stepped inside the very industry I had once admired from afar.

With the move came upgrades. No more cubicles. Each admissions advisor had their own private office. I couldn't believe it when I was assigned the corner office in the main reception lobby. I had a front-row seat to the rhythm of the city. From my window, I watched the steady stream of people walking by: shoppers, tourists, professionals, students, all dressed in their own unique styles. It was like a live fashion show every day.

Every time I stepped into the lobby, I saw anxious, wide-eyed students and their equally nervous parents waiting to be called in. I greeted them with warmth and a smile that said, "You're welcome here."

I had started to love my job. Really love it. I woke up each morning excited to get dressed, excited to get to campus. I stopped watching the clock, counting down to quitting time. I often stayed late, not because I had to, but because I wanted to. This place, this role, had lit a fire in me. I belonged here.

I spent thirty years at FIDM, and I still marvel at it. Looking back, it almost feels like a dream. I built a career in a world I had only admired from the sidelines. Over the years, I met thousands of students, many of whom left a mark on me. Some became lifelong friends. Others achieved incredible things: launching their own fashion lines, designing costumes for major productions, creating stunning interiors, or carving out names for themselves in the film and entertainment industries. Every time I saw their names in magazines, on TV credits, or heard about their latest accomplishments, I felt a deep, quiet pride. I had played a small part. I had helped open the door.

And FIDM gave so much to me in return.

Both of my daughters attended FIDM, following in my footsteps but making their own mark. Each carved out a career in the fashion industry, growing into creative forces in their own right. Eventually, they fulfilled a lifelong dream together: opening their own store.

They called it Joon, a beautiful, curated boutique nestled in the heart of North Park, San Diego. Joon isn't just a shop; it's a reflection of their shared vision. The store carries a thoughtful collection of accessories and home goods, pieces that are edgy yet refined, modern yet soulful. It's the kind of space where customers linger, drawn in by the aesthetic and held by the warmth. Watching them bring their dream to life, collaborating, building, and thriving, was one of the greatest joys of my life.

And FIDM had given them their start, too.

I had opportunities I could never have imagined: traveling across the country and around the world. New York, Hawaii, Europe. Every year I packed my bags, stepping into new cities with fresh eyes and gratitude. I stayed in five-star hotels, attended dazzling dinners, and yes, even collected a few designer handbags along the way. More than the perks, what I carried most were the relationships. Friendships formed, many lasting to this day, were some of the richest gifts of my time there. Some of those connections led to unexpected adventures, once-in-a-lifetime opportunities, and unforgettable stories, each one a thread in the tapestry of my FIDM years. Those memories deserve their own spotlight, and I'll reveal more about them in chapters to come.

CHAPTER 16
FIERCE LOVE, HARD CHOICES

I loved our little family fiercely. Kristin had arrived the year after Manny and I married, and four years later, Ashley Dawn was born, a sweet, loving child who made our family feel complete. Every day brought the kind of joy I had only imagined, the kind that makes you laugh at the smallest things and hold tight to every fleeting moment. And yet, even in the midst of that love, something still didn't feel right.

I began to notice a quiet restlessness stirring inside me. Manny was devoted and kind, endlessly planning small moments meant to delight me, but I sometimes realized I couldn't fully return the closeness he sought. I felt a tension I didn't yet understand, a gap between what my heart wanted and what my life had become. It was subtle at first, a shadow that passed quickly, but over time it became impossible to ignore.

I noticed a gradual change in myself. He sought my closeness, and sometimes I couldn't respond fully. He gave freely, hoping to spark fulfillment in me, and I tried to meet him there, but the spark I longed for wasn't always there. I felt I owed him more than I could give.

After twelve years of marriage, I made the heaviest decision of my life. I told him I wanted to separate. I'll never forget the look on his face: confusion, disbelief, then pain. He was devastated. In his mind, we were still building something together. But I wasn't, not in the way that mattered.

In Filipino culture, marriage is for life. I sometimes felt selfish, but I also saw it as an act of mercy for him, not just for me. Mom was horrified, and friends were shocked. Manny didn't stop trying. For months, he wooed me with flowers and gestures, hoping I would return, but I couldn't pretend.

The hardest part was telling Kristin and Ashley. They were eleven and seven, too young to carry such a burden, too old not to notice. We sat together, tangled in each other's arms, crying. I later pulled them aside and explained as gently as I could that it wasn't their fault or their dad's. They listened. Kristin, wise beyond her years, seemed to understand.

Later, when my mother was over with just me and the girls, she scolded me sharply. "You should just live with the way you feel. You don't throw away a marriage."

Kristin turned to her grandmother and said, "But Grandma, she's not in love."

I don't remember much else from that conversation, but I remember the pride I felt in Kristin for seeing me, really seeing me.

A year later, our divorce was finalized. There were no bitter court battles, just two people who had shared a life choosing to move forward separately with respect and grace. Remarkably, our families remained close. Manny's nieces and nephews still call me Auntie, and we are still woven into each other's lives. We never stopped being family; we just evolved into a different kind.

Even though it was the hardest decision I'd ever made, I knew it was the right one. I had chosen honesty over comfort, authenticity over pretense. And in that choice, I found a quiet strength I didn't know I had.

CHAPTER 17

KEN—THE MAN BEHIND THE SCREEN

A couple of years after my divorce, I found myself spending late nights in the strange new world of AOL chat rooms. The internet was still in its awkward teenage phase—exciting, glitchy, and unpredictable. Logging on was a ritual: that scratchy, high-pitched dial-up screech, the hopeful pause, and then the sweet sound of connection. It felt like winning a slot machine.

There were dozens of chat rooms, but let's be honest, most of us were there for the same reason: to meet someone. Public chats often turned private, a little ping popping up in the corner of the screen. It felt sneaky and thrilling, like someone pulling you aside at a crowded party to whisper, "Hey, can we talk over here?"

This was before profile pictures, so connection came through words, tone, imagination, and eventually, exchanging photos over email. That's how I met Ken.

He lived in Orange County, and after weeks of flirty late-night chats, fate intervened. My sister Jane had a conference there and invited me along. Perfect. Free hotel, mini escape. I told Ken, and we made plans to meet. He pulled up in a shiny Corvette, low, loud, and begging for attention. Dinner was elegant, the chemistry instant, the conversation easy. While Jane was busy the next day, Ken and I spent it together, laughing and exploring like we'd known each other for years.

Back home, the calls got longer, the connection deeper. He invited me for a weekend, his treat. I agreed but insisted on my own hotel. He respected that. We repeated the pattern: dinners, drinks, stories, and laughter that spilled past midnight.

Then came his next idea: "Let's drive to Vegas tomorrow," he said with a grin, "and spend the night."

It was wild but thrilling. I packed an overnight bag and left the rest at the hotel. When he pulled up the next morning, sun glinting off that Corvette, it felt like the start of a movie. The desert stretched ahead, the wind tangled my hair, and I felt deliciously alive.

We stayed at the Stratosphere, played blackjack, rode the high of his winnings, and toasted champagne at the Top of the World restaurant as Las Vegas glittered beneath us.

"You're my lucky star," he said, winking over the rim of his glass.

For a while, I believed it.

But after a few months of this, the long-distance relationship took its toll. Flights, schedules, weekends arranged around when my daughters were with their dad, it wore me down. The excitement faded, replaced by exhaustion. We already had another trip booked when I knew it was over.

I decided to go through with the visit and end it in person. That Friday, I boarded an airport shuttle, replaying the breakup speech in my head, until I noticed the man sitting across from me. I actually did a double take. He was movie-star handsome, tall, dark-haired, strong-jawed, with an easy, confident smile. He looked a lot like Pierce Brosnan, only a thousand times more handsome, and he was smiling at me.

He spoke first. "Where are you flying off to?"

"Orange County," I said, laughing, "to break up with someone."

He grinned. "Well, that's one way to start the weekend."

He wasn't flying anywhere, just taking the shuttle to pick up a friend. Odd, but intriguing. We talked the entire ride, and I found myself smiling more than I had in months. At the terminal, we said polite goodbyes. I figured that was that.

Then, sitting at my gate, I looked up. There he was again. "Fancy seeing you here," I teased.

"My friend's flight arrives at the gate next to yours," he said, sitting beside me.

We chatted for a few minutes, then my flight began boarding. As I stood, he asked, "Can I get your number? I might check in after the weekend to see if that breakup went smoothly, or if you need some moral support."

I smiled. "Sure."

I gave him my number, and as I walked down the jet bridge, I couldn't resist one last glance. He was still there, smiling, and something about it made my heart skip.

That night, after dinner with Ken, I finally said what I'd rehearsed. I cared about him, but the distance was too much. I had even changed my flight; I was leaving the next morning. He took it well. No drama, no tears, just quiet understanding.

At the airport, we hugged goodbye, grateful for what it had been, both knowing it had run its course. As I walked toward my gate, I felt a surprising peace. It wasn't heartbreak; it was release.

Not every connection is meant to last. Some simply lead you to the next chapter.

CHAPTER 18
DALE—THE ILLUSION OF US

bout a week after I got back from breaking things off with Ken, my phone rang. I picked it up without thinking.

"Hi, it's Dale. Remember me?"

I wanted to pinch myself. Dale, the impossibly handsome man from the airport shuttle. It felt like hearing from someone who only existed in a dream.

"Hello... are you there?" he asked.

"Yes! I'm here," I said quickly, trying to sound casual. "I'm just surprised to hear from you."

"Surprised? Why?"

I wanted to blurt out, "Because you look like you walked straight out of a cologne ad and you are completely out of my league." Instead, I laughed softly. "I don't know. I just didn't expect to hear from you."

He chuckled. "Well, I told you I'd call to see if your breakup went smoothly. Did it?"

"It did," I said, and just like that, we fell into an easy rhythm.

He asked if I used AOL. "Of course," I told him.

"Great. Let's chat on there. I'll create a private room. Just for us."

After we hung up, we both dialed into AOL, waiting through the screech and hum of the modem. We met in a private room he created. He called it Labyrinth, which felt mysterious and poetic.

We sat behind our screens, fingers tapping, sharing pieces of ourselves in a space that felt like a secret world. It was oddly romantic, like passing handwritten notes under a table, one line at a time.

I told him about my recent divorce, my daughters, and my work at FIDM. He was fascinated, especially with my job. Then he casually mentioned he had been a professional model. I wasn't surprised. He added that he was recently on the cover of *Men's Fitness* magazine.

I laughed. "I wish I could've seen that."

"I can send it to you," he said.

A moment later, I heard the ding of a new email. The download took ages, but when the image finally appeared, I could hardly breathe.

There he was, centered on the cover of *Men's Fitness* in boxer shorts, his bare chest sculpted and gleaming like it had been kissed by the sun and polished for the gods. He didn't just look beautiful. He radiated confidence and effortless allure.

And now he was talking to me.

After we logged off, we talked more on the phone. His voice was low and soothing; the kind you could listen to for hours. He told me he was a Buddhist and a vegetarian, that he had recently moved to the Bay Area from the East Coast, and that he worked as a video game developer. Smart, creative, and stunning. He was starting to feel like a character written too perfectly to be real.

We agreed to meet for dinner later that week.

As the night approached, my nerves kicked in hard. I must have tried on ten outfits. Then came the shoes. He was tall, maybe six foot one or two, so I knew I could wear any heel I wanted, which somehow made choosing even harder.

Twenty minutes into the drive, something felt off. I glanced down and gasped.

Two different shoes. Completely different pairs.

I turned the car around, cursing the whole way. This was pre cell phone days, so there was no way to call or text. No shoe emergency excuse. Just me, my mismatched heels, and rising panic.

Back home, I swapped shoes and ran out again, fighting back tears. *He is not going to wait for me,* I thought. A man who looked like that had options, surely.

Forty minutes later, I burst into the Sir Francis Drake Hotel lobby, my heart hammering, breaths coming in short, sharp gasps. There he was, sitting calmly, like he had stepped off a film set. Gosh, he really looked like Pierce Brosnan, but better. When he saw me, he smiled and rose.

"Hey, there you are."

He had waited.

Every ounce of panic, every frantic thought, evaporated. Relief flooded through me. Gratitude warmed my chest. And in that instant, a spark of something hopeful ignited, tiny but unstoppable.

We began seeing each other regularly after that. Soon, Dale found an apartment a few blocks from where I worked, right in the heart of the Tenderloin. Not the safest neighborhood, but convenient. I would park in the garage near work and walk five blocks to his place, clutching my purse tightly at night. During the day it almost felt pleasant. Eventually, I stopped flinching at the sirens.

Dale lived simply, almost monastically. He had once spent two years in silence at a Buddhist monastery, and his apartment reflected that calm. No clutter, no excess. He wore neutral clothing, avoided leather, and didn't own a car. So I was always the one behind the wheel, but I didn't mind.

One afternoon he took me to meet friends who had come to San Francisco to see the Dalai Lama speak. We spent the day watching old videos of the Dalai Lama, like kids hyping up for a concert. Everyone was gentle and open-hearted. For someone who had once graced a *Men's Fitness* cover, he lived with surprising humility.

Eventually, he brought up something I had been dreading. Meeting my daughters. Ashley and Kristin were only eight and twelve and had not seen me with another man since the divorce. I worried about protecting their hearts, but Dale was gentle.

"We will take it slow," he said.

We went to the zoo and the day went smoothly. He made them laugh and even hoisted little Ashley onto his shoulders. Watching her giggle made my heart swell. Later, he and Kristin roller skated at the beach while Ashley and I watched from the sand, smiling as the sun began to set.

Afterward, we walked along the shoreline. The girls skipped ahead, their laughter carried by the breeze. Dale slipped his hand into mine and said quietly, "I really enjoy spending time with you and with them." Before I could answer, he leaned down and kissed me.

The girls turned around smirking and giggling, though I sensed a flicker of discomfort. That night we talked it through. They admitted it felt strange but said they were okay as long as they still came first. I assured them they always would.

A few weeks later, I invited Dale out with my sister Jane and my nieces for a night of dancing. We took him to one of my old post-divorce hangouts, loud and pulsing with music.

Dale, after two years of monastery quiet, could not handle it. He sat with his head in his hands. It was sensory overload, so we left early.

On the walk to my car, one of my nieces suggested hitting a gay club in the Castro. Before I could respond, Dale lit up. "That sounds great," he said.

At the club, he seemed completely at home. The noise didn't bother him at all. Tall and striking, he drew attention instantly. Even while dancing with me, guys tried to squeeze between us. Jane and I pretended to be a couple to fend off attention and laughed about it. Still, later that night I couldn't help wondering why the noise hadn't bothered him there. I didn't ask.

About six months into our relationship, we were having dinner when he said he had a confession.

My stomach sank. Confession was never a good word.

He paused, looked down, and said, "There's something I should have told you earlier."

A chill moved through me.

He told me he had an ex-fiancée.

They had broken up shortly before we met, as in days before. In fact, she was the person he had gone to the airport to meet that day. She was flying in to collect her things. He hadn't mentioned it because, according to him, "it didn't seem important."

I sat there frozen. But he wasn't finished.

He explained that both their families, prominent Ivy League types, had been expecting a wedding. Their parents still didn't even know the engagement was off. Now his parents were coming to town.

"And?" I asked.

"Well," he said hesitantly, "my ex and I are going to pretend we are still engaged. Just for the weekend. To keep up appearances."

I stared at him, feeling like I had been punched. He kept talking, trying to smooth it over, but all I heard was the roar of betrayal.

He swore it was over between them. He said he cared deeply for me. He often reminded me how much he loved me, how much he cared for me, and I clung to those words. But how could that be true if he was still playing make-believe with someone else right in front of his family?

No matter how gently he tried to say it, I couldn't make sense of any of it. All I could feel was the truth, sharp and silent: I wasn't part of the picture he showed to the people who mattered most. And that hurt more than anything he said.

Yet after that strange weekend, after he played fiancé for his parents, Dale called me first thing Monday morning. His voice was soft and apologetic. He said he was sorry for hurting me and promised that he and his ex would break the news to their parents sometime soon.

Sometime soon. What did that even mean?

But I didn't push. Part of me was terrified that asking too much would send him running.

As conflicted as I was, I wasn't ready to let go. I was still under his spell, this tall, striking, spiritually centered man who roller skated to work, once lived in silence, and kissed me softly on the beach while my daughters looked on. So I forgave him, or pretended to. We picked up where we left off, as if there weren't cracks already forming beneath our feet.

I spent more and more of my free time with him. His apartment, tucked into the grittiest corner of the Tenderloin, became a second home. Despite the sirens and shouting outside, it was where I wanted to be.

One Saturday, I showed up to find him in tears.

"Dale? What's wrong?"

He looked up, eyes red. "Didn't you hear? Gianni's dead. He was murdered."

At first, I was confused. Then it clicked. Gianni Versace, the famous designer, had been shot that morning. I had seen the news, but I was stunned by Dale's reaction. He spoke about Gianni as if they had been close friends. He didn't offer details, but his grief was raw. I didn't know how to question it without seeming cold.

So I comforted him. We ordered takeout. I kept myself busy with paperwork while he tinkered with one of his game prototypes, quiet and distant.

By the next morning, it was as if nothing had happened. He greeted me with a smile and a bowl of Trader Joe's Vanilla Clusters cereal, our favorite breakfast since we'd been together. Not one mention of Gianni.

The emotional pendulum swings were starting to make me wonder. One day he was overcome with tears; the next, he was laughing as if everything was fine. Still, I stayed. I kept telling myself there was more good than bad. He continued to tell me how much he loved me, how much he cared, and I grasped them, desperate for the comfort they offered. I didn't realize I was slowly erasing my own boundaries, softening them with every "maybe" and every "it's not that big a deal."

But something about that weekend stayed with me, not just the grief, but how quickly it vanished. I should have seen the red flags waving right in front of me.

Deep down, I wondered if we were even compatible and questioned whether we shared enough of the same interests. He didn't have a car, so I did all the driving. And I found myself wishing for someone who could simply show up for me, keys in hand, ready to take me somewhere for once.

Instead, I was always navigating the gridlock of the Tenderloin, weaving past sidewalks littered with needles and panhandlers. Every time I walked those five blocks from the garage, I was greeted by chaos.

Still, I stayed.

Something about Dale kept me hanging on. Maybe it was his beauty. Maybe it was the fantasy. I wondered if I was in love with him or the idea of him. Was he an accessory, a striking handbag you carry to feel a little more special? Maybe. I wasn't sure. I only knew I wanted so badly for this to work that I kept convincing myself it would.

I even invited him to FIDM's celebration dinner in Beverly Hills, an elegant black-tie event. I asked if he owned a black suit. He said he actually had a tuxedo. I was thrilled. The thought of arriving with him on my arm, turning heads among the admissions staff, made me giddy. It felt like a debut.

But a couple of weeks before the event, he broke my heart.

We were at his apartment. It was just another ordinary evening, or so I thought, until he turned to me, solemn and soft-spoken, and said, "I think our relationship has run its course."

My stomach dropped.

Then, as casually as if he were telling me what he had for lunch, he said he had met someone else. Her name was Maria. He had met her on the train, of all places, on his morning commute to work.

I couldn't help but laugh bitterly. "Wow. Is this your thing? Meeting your next girlfriend between transit stops?" After all, we had met on a shuttle.

He smiled faintly but didn't respond.

He told me he still cared about me and valued the year we had spent together, but it was time to move on. Then, without missing a beat, he said he still wanted to go to Beverly Hills with me for the celebration dinner. He said Maria already knew and was fine with it. He would still love to be my date—if I let him.

The audacity.

The strange thing was, I let him.

I still wanted that grand entrance with him, even though I knew it would be our last. That is how far down the rabbit hole I had gone, so eager to preserve the illusion, so desperate not to feel discarded, that I let a man who had just dumped me escort me like a prize pony.

We checked into our hotel the afternoon of the event. When we got to our room, he realized he had forgotten dress socks. Of course he had. He rushed back out to find a pair. I had no doubt the errand included a detour to a pay phone so he could check in with Maria, his actual girlfriend.

Still, we made an entrance. As we walked into the private dining room of the upscale Beverly Hills restaurant, arm in arm, heads turned. We were a striking pair, and I basked in it, knowing it was fleeting.

Co-workers from other campuses came up to greet us. Some were even flirtatious. I loved it. I soaked it in, fully aware it would never happen again.

Once seated, the waiter brought out tiny bowls of broth to stimulate the palate. Dale immediately began questioning the ingredients. Was it vegetable based? Any animal stock? When assured there would be vegetarian options for the entrée, he still pressed on. I could feel polite smiles tightening around the table. The sparkle of our entrance began to dim.

Aside from that awkward exchange, dinner was delicious. Afterward, we listened to a short speech from our college president and even danced a little. It was surreal and bittersweet, but oddly nice.

Back at the hotel, I asked what he wanted to do the next day. Our flight wasn't until the evening. He suggested Venice Beach and maybe Rodeo Drive if there was time.

"We will have time for both if we start early," I said.

The next morning, we caught a bus to Venice Beach. It was a beautiful day. We strolled the boardwalk, ducked into quirky shops, watched bodybuilders at Muscle Beach, and walked barefoot in the sand. For a few hours, we were almost like a real couple. Almost.

Later, we caught another bus back to Beverly Hills. On the ride, an older man sitting across from us kept glancing between us. Suddenly he looked straight at me and said with conviction, "This guy is madly in love with you. He will treat you like a queen. Don't ever let him go."

I nearly laughed.

Dale smiled and murmured something under his breath, but I didn't ask him to repeat it. I didn't need to. The irony was loud enough.

In the end, it was a good trip, a strange little farewell breakup vacation. Awkward at times, but also fun in a disconnected way. More importantly, it gave me clarity. Breaking up, however much it stung, was probably for the best.

But the sting lingered. I wasn't sure what hurt more: that he met someone else, that he ended things, or that I had been so in love with the idea of a relationship that didn't even exist. Maybe I wasn't in love with him. Maybe I was in love with the idea of being loved by someone beautiful and broken in just the right way. But regardless, my heart was aching.

Dale was never mine to keep. And I wondered if there would ever be someone who would fill the void I longed to have filled, or if I simply wasn't deserving of that kind of love.

CHAPTER 19
SECOND KIDNAPPING

The Night Begins

I thought heartbreak hurt the most—that evening would prove me wrong.

It was Wednesday, April 15, 1998. I was thirty-eight. Kristin was thirteen, Ashley just nine. Not long before, I had been dumped by Dale, and the sting of that ended relationship was still fresh. I had promised Ashley I would be home in time to help her make flan for her school's international potluck the next day. She was thrilled. We had planned it together, and I told her, "Don't worry, Ash, I'll be back in time." I meant every word.

That night, FIDM's admissions department hosted a mini celebration to mark the successful start of the spring quarter. We left campus around 6:30 and walked a couple of blocks through Union Square to the Sir Francis Drake Hotel. The Starlight Room glittered atop the building, offering sweeping views of the city. I only had time for a glass of wine and a few bites of hors d'oeuvres, but I was glad I went. Laughter and relief hung in the air, a soft feeling of accomplishment settling over all of us.

Then I glanced at the time. It was already a little past 7:30. I was running behind.

I said my goodbyes, gave quick hugs, and walked briskly the two blocks to the BART station. The platform buzzed with its usual weeknight chaos. I caught the train and rode the familiar thirty-five minutes to my stop in El Cerrito, already mapping out the steps of the flan recipe in my head. I wanted to be home, in the kitchen, with my daughter.

When the train doors opened, I stepped off, rode the escalator to street level, and crossed to the overflow parking lot across the street, the unattended outdoor lot where I had parked countless times. I remember holding my keys in my hand, walking with purpose, already halfway home in my mind.

Then everything changed.

The Abduction

As I opened the car door, I was grabbed from behind, an arm locking around me with brutal force. Then I felt it, a cold blade pressed to my neck, sharp and unforgiving. My body jolted with fear.

He shoved me into the driver's seat with a violence that stole my breath. The knife pushed harder against my skin as he ordered me to climb over to the passenger side. My mind spun, my body trembled, but I moved. I was fit enough, flexible enough, but nothing on earth prepares you for this.

No. Not again. This could not be happening *again.*

I did not think. I reacted. As he reached for the ignition, I flung the door open, threw myself out of the car, and ran.

But he was fast.

I heard his footsteps right behind me. I tried to scream, desperate and wild, but just like the last time, nothing came out. My voice was gone. My legs were moving, but inside, I felt frozen.

He caught me and shoved me hard to the ground. "You bitches are all alike," he snarled.

What did that even mean?

My face scraped across sharp, uneven cobblestones. My skin burned. He rolled me over and struck me once, then again. My vision blurred. My mouth filled with the taste of blood and rising panic.

Then he grabbed my purse. It was a thick woven Sak bag, sturdy and heavy. The strap wrapped around my neck like a rope. He dragged me across the gravel by it, choking me with each step. I clawed at the strap, trying to wedge my fingers under it, desperate for air.

When he dragged me back to the car, he wasted no time. Another blow landed against my face. Hard. Fast. Then another. And another. The world tilted. Pain burst through my skull in hot, blinding flashes. I could not think. I could not breathe. My body folded in on itself, and everything inside me dimmed.

I came to with a throbbing ache pounding through my skull. My face felt warm and wet, and when I touched it, my fingers came away red. *Blood.* Not again. Just like before.

I blinked, trying to clear the haze from my eyes, but the pain only throbbed harder. My head felt split open, and the world around me blurred into shapes and shadows. Then I realized we were moving. He was driving. I could feel the vibration of the road through the floorboard, hear the steady hum of the tires cutting through the night.

I turned my head slowly, each muscle screaming in protest, and looked at him.

There he was. His hands steady on the wheel, his face flat and unreadable.

"What do you want?" I managed, my voice cracked and unfamiliar. "Where are you taking me?"

I was stunned the words came out at all. Last time, fear had stolen my voice completely. But this time, even through the terror, something inside me pushed the words up and out.

He didn't answer. Not even a glance.

But he didn't need to speak. I saw the only thing that mattered: in his gloved right hand, gripping it tightly while steering with the other, was a blade. Gleaming under the faint dashboard glow. A silver box cutter. Thick and industrial, made for slicing through carpet or metal, not flesh.

The silence between us grew heavier, pressing against my chest.

And in that suffocating stillness, the truth settled over me: I was trapped in a nightmare that had returned for me. A nightmare I had barely survived the first time.

The farther we drove, the darker everything became. Streetlights thinned, buildings dissolved into silhouettes, and the city faded into deserted industrial streets. Warehouses. Chain-link fences. Empty lots stretching out like dead land.

Still, he said nothing.

I glanced down at my watch. A little after nine.

The panic hit me so hard it felt like my stomach flipped. *The girls.*

Kristin was old enough to stay with Ashley, but I never stayed out this late on a school night. They hadn't eaten yet. I just knew it. Ashley would be waiting, flan recipe in small hands, pacing the kitchen, checking the clock, wondering why I wasn't home.

I imagined their faces pressed to the window, searching for headlights that wouldn't come. That thought gutted me.

The Assault

Then, without warning, he pulled the car over.

The engine cut. The headlights clicked off. Darkness swallowed us whole. The streets were completely deserted. We were in an industrial wasteland.

Empty lots stretched on either side, dark warehouses looming like silent sentinels. No cars passed, no streetlights lit the pavement, only shadows and the oppressive stillness of a place where nothing human should linger.

My heart lurched into my throat. The silence wasn't empty anymore. It felt charged, electric, waiting.

He still didn't speak. He didn't need to. I knew why we were there. I knew exactly what was coming. I was about to experience a violation deeper and more devastating than anything I had ever endured, and that is saying something. Because I had been violated before. But this felt different. This felt final.

For the first time, I truly believed I was not going to survive.

I broke. Sobs tore out of me as I begged. "Please, take my wallet. Take the car. Please just let me go."

He said nothing.

Then he leaned over and climbed on top of me with a violent force that knocked the air out of me.

He pushed the seat back as far as it would go. I froze, my eyes fixed on the blade inches from my face.

For the first time, I saw his features clearly. Late twenties, maybe early thirties. Brown skin. Dark, messy hair. His expression was flat, almost vacant, yet strangely focused. Like he wasn't really there. Like he was acting out a script written somewhere deep in his own darkness.

I kicked and twisted beneath him, throwing every ounce of strength I had into fighting him off. I screamed, or tried to, but the sound came out fractured. I felt the blade press into my cheek, slicing through my skin, warning me what defiance would cost.

Still, I fought.

But he was stronger. His hands roamed roughly over my entire body, gripping, pressing, and asserting control, leaving me helpless beneath him. Then he yanked my pants and underwear down in one brutal movement. The sound that will echo in my nightmares forever followed: the slow, deliberate pull of his zipper. That sound told me there would be no mercy.

He forced himself inside me.

Something in me snapped. My mind couldn't hold the reality of what was happening. The pain, the terror, the violation. It was too much for one body, one heart.

So I disappeared.

It felt like I floated above myself, watching from somewhere far away. Watching a woman I didn't recognize being hurt in ways that shattered my understanding of cruelty. I wanted to reach down and pull her out. I wanted to save her.

But I couldn't reach her.

Because she was me.

I could see my body pinned beneath him, unmoving. I could hear the dull, wet sounds. Feel the rough rhythm. But it was all happening from a distance.

I was screaming on the inside, but nothing came out. My throat clenched shut. I couldn't breathe. Couldn't cry. Couldn't make a sound.

It was as if I had slipped through some crack in the floor of reality, and now I was trapped in some inescapable nightmare that wasn't a nightmare at all. It was real. It was happening. And I couldn't stop it.

A thousand thoughts raced through my mind in a storm of disbelief and horror.

How is this happening?

Why me, again?

Did I do something to deserve this?

Is there a sign on me that says, "Take me, break me, ruin me"?

Shame settled into my chest like wet cement, heavy and suffocating, impossible to shake. I hated him, yes, but in that moment, I also hated myself.

Not just in the fleeting way you hate yourself when you feel powerless or afraid, but in a way that would cling to me long after that night was over. I didn't know it yet, but I would carry this moment like a wound that never truly closed. I would question everything, my choices, my worth, my very existence.

That night would burrow its way into my soul. And in the months and years that followed, I would come to blame myself for surviving it. For not escaping sooner. For all the bad things that had happened in my life. I would end up hating myself.

I felt weak. Dirty. Ashamed. Like somehow this was my fault.

I had been beaten before. I had known pain, humiliation, and cruelty, but this… this was a different kind of destruction.

It wasn't just my body being violated. It was my spirit. My very sense of self.

It felt like he was reaching inside me, ripping apart everything I thought I was, everything I had fought to become, everything I had already survived. He was tearing down the last walls I had built to protect myself from the world, and I didn't know if there would be anything left of me when he was done.

Then headlights appeared behind us. A car pulled up and parked, its lights staying on. He froze. Then in a flash, he scrambled back into the driver's seat and started the car. He didn't speak. He just drove.

We stayed in that maze of dark, abandoned streets, and my heart raced with a sickening realization. He wasn't done. He hadn't finished. And I knew he was going to try again.

But I couldn't let that happen. I couldn't survive it a second time.

So I did the only thing I could. I clenched my fist and punched him, hard, across the side of his face.

The car jerked and swerved wildly. He snapped his head toward me, eyes burning, and raised the blade. He slashed at me, aiming to stab.

I threw up my arms, blocking, twisting, swinging wildly. The blade caught my arms, my hands, my face again and again, carving deep, burning cuts I couldn't even feel in the chaos.

But I kept fighting, because if he was going to rape me again, he would have to kill me first.

My adrenaline was on fire, flooding every nerve like a blaze I couldn't control. I felt no pain, only purpose. I wasn't thinking. I was surviving. I had already been broken once that night, but not again. Not this time.

If he tried to touch me again, he was going to have to fight for it. I was done being a victim. I was done being silent. I would rather die than let him violate me again.

Then we crashed.

The Crash / 911

The sound was deafening. Glass. Metal. Screams, maybe his, maybe mine. Time seemed to stop. I slammed against the dashboard, hard. No airbags back then to cushion the blow. My skull rattled, and for a moment, everything blurred. I could taste blood in my mouth and feel it trickling from my forehead, hot and sticky. My arms stung and burned, sliced open in the struggle. I looked over. He wasn't moving. Not right away.

We had crashed into what looked like an iron fence, jagged and twisted around the front of the car like a steel web. The engine sputtered, then went silent. He tried shifting gears, jamming the stick like that would force the car back to life, but it was dead. We were done.

Then he moved. Slowly. Groggily. He pushed the driver's door open, staggered out, and took off into the night, disappearing like a shadow swallowed by darkness.

I was in shock, drenched in blood, my face pulsing with pain, trembling with disbelief, but somehow my hands moved on their own. I managed to pull my pants up, not even understanding how my body was still functioning. I fumbled through my bag and found my flip phone, the keys sticky from my blood. I flipped it open, my fingers barely working, and dialed.

911.

It rang once. Twice. Three times.

Then, "911, please hold."

Hold?

What the actual *fuck*?

I could feel myself slipping, the adrenaline wearing off and the pain creeping in like a slow flood. My vision was blurring. My body felt heavy. I was crashing inside and out.

When the dispatcher finally came on, their voice sounded miles away. "What's your emergency?"

I choked on the words. "I've been abducted… he crashed the car… he ran off…" Everything spilled out in gasps, my breath shaking.

"Are you hurt?"

"I… I don't think so," I said, because I couldn't feel anything. My body was numb, buzzing with leftover adrenaline. "But I'm bleeding. My face… my hands…" I looked down and only then really saw the blood.

"What's your location?"

Of course. I should have expected that. But my mind was spiraling, the streets around me unfamiliar and warped by shock.

"I don't know!" I screamed, panic detonating all over again. "I don't fucking know!"

"Ma'am, I need you to calm down and take a deep breath."

I snapped. "Why don't you calm down? I was just kidnapped and almost killed—just get me the hell out of here!"

"We will. I promise. But I need something, anything, to find you. Can you step outside and tell me what you see? A landmark, a sign, anything," the dispatcher said gently. "We need a location."

"I can't, I can't go out there," I whispered, voice cracking.

I looked around. The adrenaline was back. My heart raced. I had locked the doors the second he fled, and going back out there felt like suicide. What if he was still lurking in the shadows?

"Okay. Then look out your windows. Anything, street signs, buildings, landmarks?"

I forced myself to focus, squinting through the smeared windshield and the blood in my eyes. My breath hitched.

"There's… there's a freeway overpass. I think we're in Richmond. It's dark, industrial. I see a mortuary sign down the block." It sounded insane. Like a horror movie. But it was real.

"Stay on the line, help is on the way."

And then, finally, sirens.

Faint at first. Then louder. Closer. Real.

Red and blue lights sliced through the dark, bouncing off metal and concrete. Two police cruisers pulled up, followed by an ambulance. I sagged back against the seat, my body shaking, my hands still wrapped around the phone like it was the only thing keeping me upright.

I was safe.

At least for now.

But I knew the real pain was only just beginning.

A police officer approached my Camry, flashlight beam bouncing off the shattered glass and twisted metal. He tapped gently on the window, startling me. I had forgotten I locked the doors. I stared at him, unsure. My brain knew he was a cop, but my body didn't trust anyone, not yet.

He held up a hand. "Ma'am, it's the police. You're safe now. Please open the door."

Safe.

The word felt foreign. Unreal. Like a lie.

I couldn't move. My body was frozen, suspended between panic and exhaustion. My fingers trembled as I slowly reached for the lock. The door clicked open with a reluctant thud.

He took one look at me and flinched. "Medic!" he shouted over his shoulder.

I must have looked like something out of a horror movie, my face a swollen, bloodied mess, my arms streaked in crimson, my shirt torn and stained.

Everything blurred after that.

Hands reached in. Gentle hands. They moved me with care, strapping me to a stretcher. I remember cold wipes on my skin, the sting of antiseptic in my wounds, voices trying to soothe me. My limbs were numb, my mind spinning, detached.

A different officer stepped close, his voice soft but urgent. "Can you tell me what happened?"

I tried. I gave him fragments. Words. The shape of a nightmare. I couldn't speak in full sentences. I barely had enough strength to breathe. But he listened. I could see in his eyes he understood more than my words were saying.

Then it hit me.

"My kids," I gasped. "Please, my daughters. Someone has to tell my girls I'm okay…"

He crouched lower, nodding. "We'll take care of them. Who can we call?"

"My sister… Joji. Please tell her to go to them." I gave him my flip phone. He found her number and walked away while speaking to her.

There were two attendants in the back of the ambulance with me. They hovered over my body, tending to the bleeding, gently wiping at the wounds on my arms and face. I could see their lips moving, see the concern in their eyes, but it was like watching a silent film. Their voices didn't reach me. I was floating, somewhere above, somewhere outside myself, watching a scene I couldn't stop or fully enter.

The Hospital

It wasn't until we reached the emergency room and the gurney rolled through the automatic doors that one voice finally broke through the fog. A nurse rushed to my side, and as her eyes scanned my battered face and blood-soaked shirt, she gasped, not softly, not professionally, but like a horrified mother.

"Oh my Jesus," she cried. "What did they do to you, baby?"

Her words hit like a bolt of lightning. I can still hear her voice, echoing in my head, years later. That was the moment the tears came again, heavy and uncontrollable. Something about the way she said it made it real. It made me real.

After they got me into a hospital gown, another nurse, gentle and soft-spoken, came in to soothe me. She sat at the edge of the bed, touched my arm carefully, and asked as kindly and compassionately as she could, "Sweetheart, did he sexually assault you in any way?"

Without hesitation, I shook my head and said, "No."

The lie came so fast it startled even me. But there was no way I could say it out loud. No way I could let those words exist in the room. If I did, then that part of the kidnapping would become real. And I wasn't ready for that.

I wasn't ready for the disgust I felt crawling under my skin. I wasn't ready for the shame cemented in my chest. I wasn't ready to admit that I had become the kind of woman I never thought I would be, one who felt tainted, soiled, used.

Moments later, a police officer entered the room. He looked young, calm, with kind eyes and a quiet manner. He apologized for having to question me and assured me they were doing everything they could to find the man who did this.

I nodded, still numb. They gave me water and crackers. I hadn't realized how starving I was, how empty my body felt, until I began eating. But the nausea crept in as quickly as the crumbs fell. My stomach turned violently the moment my mind drifted to what really happened.

I told the officer what I could.

How I was attacked in the parking lot. How he strangled me with my own purse and knocked me out cold. How I woke up in a moving car and panicked when I realized we were heading deeper and deeper into the vacant industrial parts of Richmond. How I fought him, punched him, clawed at him. How he slashed at me with the blade in his hand.

But I didn't tell him everything.

I left out the worst of it. I couldn't speak it. The words were stuck in my throat like thorns. Saying them would make it real. Saying them would confirm that I had lost something I could never get back.

So I said nothing.

I kept that part buried deep.

I felt dirty, like it was my fault, like I somehow deserved it.

And that night, I made a decision.

This secret would be mine.

And it would go with me to the grave.

Jane Arrives / The Mirror

Joji must have called my other sister, Jane, because not long after, she arrived at the hospital with her fiancé, John. I wasn't in my room when they got there. I had finally mustered the strength to go to the bathroom, dragging myself slowly down the hallway, still dazed and aching in places I couldn't even feel yet.

That was when I ran into Jane.

She saw me before I saw her. Her face crumpled instantly, and the tears came without warning. “Oh my God,” she whispered, “What happened to you?”

But I didn’t stop walking. I couldn’t.

Shame flooded every part of me. I was embarrassed. Disgusted. I could barely face myself. How could I face her?

It felt like déjà vu, an emotional mirror of that first time, years ago, after my kidnapping at Harrah’s. Back then, it was Ester who had found me in the casino bathroom. And just like then, I bolted. I pushed open the door to the hospital restroom and locked it behind me like my life depended on it.

And that was when I saw myself.

Really saw myself.

I stepped slowly toward the mirror, and the image staring back knocked the wind out of me. It was worse than Harrah’s. So much worse.

My face was a patchwork of bruises and bandages, the cuts still raw and angry underneath. My arms were wrapped in gauze, dotted with dried blood. My eyes were swollen, not just from the attack, but from everything. From what I couldn’t say out loud.

But then I saw it.

The ring around my neck.

A deep, angry red. A rope-like bruise from my own purse strap where he had strangled me. The imprint was so defined, it looked like someone had tried to brand me. And in some ways, they had.

I stared at it. Frozen. Horrified.

That mark would stay with me for the next six months, fading slowly, like a cruel countdown. Each time I looked in the mirror, it reminded me of that night. Of him. Of what he did to me. And worse, of what I hadn't told anyone.

There was no denying what had happened. Not now.

It was carved into my skin.

Proof I couldn't erase.

Shame I couldn't wash off.

And a grief that would take years, maybe a lifetime, to understand.

I finally left the bathroom.

I didn't say a word, just collapsed into Jane's arms, and we both cried. No explanations, no details. Just sobs and the trembling warmth of someone who loved me, holding on like she could keep me from falling apart completely.

I told them what I could. Just enough to get through the conversation. Just enough to make it through the rest of the night. I still left the worst part buried inside me, tucked behind trembling lips and locked behind shame.

When the doctor finally released me, all I wanted was to get home and feel safe again. Jane had brought me a change of clothes, thank God, because the police kept the ones I'd arrived in as evidence. They said they would be tested for the guy's DNA in case he had bled during the struggle. The idea of him bleeding on me made my stomach turn.

As eager as I was to go home, I was also terrified.

Terrified of what I would see in my daughters' eyes.

Terrified of how I would explain any of this.

Terrified that I was about to relive it all, second by second, through their pain.

Going Home

Jane and John drove me home in silence. We moved slowly toward the front door, like every step carried the weight of what had just happened. I wasn't sure if I was walking toward safety or shame.

Before we even reached the porch, the door swung open. It was Erika, my niece. Her face was pale, her eyes wide. Joji and Erika had come to stay with the girls the moment they got the call from the police.

And then Kristin and Ashley. They ran toward me, arms outstretched, and wrapped themselves around me like they were afraid I'd disappear again. Their touch was light, gentle, careful not to hurt me, but even that tenderness shattered me. I cried harder than I had all night.

They shouldn't have had to see me like that. I was their mother, supposed to protect them, not come home broken and bleeding.

Before I could even sit down, I told them I needed to take a shower. I had to wash him off me. It wasn't even a want; it was a primal need. I didn't care how exhausted I was or how much my body ached. I couldn't feel like myself again until I scrubbed every trace of him from my skin.

No one questioned it. They just let me go. They understood. Or at least they tried to. When I emerged, hair wrapped in towel and fresh clothes, they were all waiting, quiet, hovering, trying to be helpful without crowding me. "Do you want something to eat?" they asked softly.

I shook my head. No. My stomach was a tangled knot of nausea and sorrow. I would have just thrown it up anyway.

But water, I needed water. I drank so much of it, I felt like I was trying to drown something in me. Maybe I was.

As I sat there, hair still dripping, body bruised, wrapped in the warmth of home but still shivering inside, I looked at my daughters. Their eyes said everything—worry, confusion, fear, and so much love. That's when the guilt settled in like fog. How could I do this to them? How could I let them see me like this? How could I be so careless, so stupid? I blamed myself for all of it. And as much as they needed comfort, in that moment I didn't feel like I deserved to give it. I had survived something horrific, but all I could think about was how I had failed them.

That night, no one wanted to be alone. Everyone stayed with us. It was like our little house had turned into a quiet sanctuary where fear huddled beside love, and no one dared to leave.

The girls insisted on sleeping in my bed with me. Their small bodies curled up on either side of mine like bookends, holding me together when I felt like I was falling apart. Joji and Erika made beds for themselves on the floor beside us; they didn't want to leave our side. Not even for a minute.

Even Jane and John stayed. It was already late, and they lived about thirty miles away, but none of us wanted to say goodbye. The thought of separating felt unbearable.

That night, the house was filled with soft breathing, quiet sobs, and the heavy silence of people who had seen too much in a single day.

I lay in bed staring at the ceiling, one daughter tucked under each arm, listening to the fragile rhythm of their sleep.

And I wondered, *Would they ever feel safe again?*

The Next Morning

The next morning, John had to leave early for work. He was a firefighter, and his shift couldn't wait. His commute was about forty-five minutes. The rest of the house stayed quiet, cloaked in a tender, watchful calm. Joji, Jane, and Erika stayed home with me along with the girls, refusing to leave our side. No one was in a rush to return to their lives just yet. We were all still suspended in the aftermath, trying to make sense of what had happened.

I remember waking up feeling like I had been hit by a truck. My head throbbed with a dull, relentless ache, and nausea churned in my stomach like a storm. I apologized profusely to Ashley, still weighed down by the memory of that silly little flan. "I'm so sorry I wasn't home in time to help you," I told her, my voice barely steady.

But she just hugged me, her eyes full of love and relief. "I'm just happy you came home," she whispered. That nearly broke me.

One of my sisters called my primary care physician, just like the hospital had instructed, and they insisted I come in immediately. Joji's son, my nephew John-John, drove me gently, treating me like I was made of glass. I guess in some ways, I was. Fortunately, all my cuts and wounds were superficial, painful, but nothing that wouldn't heal on its own. My doctor confirmed what we already suspected: a severe concussion. I needed rest. Close monitoring. No stress. As if that were even possible.

Joji called FIDM and spoke to my director, carefully threading her words to protect my privacy. Then she called our mom, who was vacationing in the Philippines at the time. She softened the story the best she could, sparing her the raw horror of it. Jane called my brother Jun and his wife Ingrid, who in turn began quietly spreading the word to the rest of the family.

Within days, cards and flowers began pouring in. Friends dropped by with meals and hugs and warm, searching eyes. They didn't know what to say and, truthfully, neither did I. I felt so much love, and yet, I also felt something darker. Something I couldn't shake.

Guilt.

I didn't know exactly why, but it was suffocating. As if somehow I didn't deserve the kindness. As if I had invited all this pain into my life. I hated feeling that way, but it had already taken root.

And I knew then this wasn't over. The physical wounds would eventually heal. But the real ones? The ones no one could see? Those were only just beginning to form.

The Detective

That afternoon, a detective showed up at my house. I opened the door cautiously, still sore, still jumpy. But the moment I saw him, something in me relaxed. He had kind eyes and a calm energy that immediately put me at ease. Oddly enough, he was the spitting image of Sean Penn. Same intense stare, same slightly disheveled hair, same soulful expression. He smiled gently and introduced himself, then stepped inside.

It turned out he lived in Benicia, just like I did, but he worked as a detective for the El Cerrito Police Department. He and his wife even owned a family gym in town. Somehow, that little piece of information made me trust him even more. He wasn't just some stranger doing his job. He was part of the community. My community.

From the start, I felt strangely comfortable around him. Maybe it was the way he carried himself, firm but kind. Or maybe it was how visibly angry and heartbroken he seemed about what had happened to me. He didn't hide it. In fact, he told me directly that he had three daughters of his own, and this case hit him hard.

"This one's personal," he said. His voice cracked slightly when he said it.

He asked if I could come down to the El Cerrito police station the next day to look through mugshots and work with a sketch artist. I hesitated. The last time I did that in Reno, it had been a humiliating, traumatizing disaster. But he gently assured me that things had changed since then. Everything was computerized now, much faster, much more efficient, and far less invasive.

I agreed.

The next day, Joji's husband drove me to the station. The detective, who I was already mentally calling Officer Sean Penn, greeted me and led me to his office. I couldn't help but laugh softly when I noticed his walls were plastered with magazine clippings and photos of the real Sean Penn.

He saw me looking and grinned. "The guys at the station tease me nonstop about it," he said. "Even my kids are in on it."

His lightness helped. I liked him. I trusted him. But not enough to tell him the whole truth. Not yet. That part of my story, the real part, was still too raw, too shameful. It stayed locked inside me, hidden behind bandages and bruises and polite nods.

He introduced me to the sketch artist, who, thank God, was nothing like the one in Reno. This man was warm, respectful, and he didn't make me feel like I was being judged or interrogated. With the help of a computer, we worked efficiently and managed to put together a sketch that I felt was accurate, at least as accurate as my battered memory would allow.

Before I left, the detective handed me a small slip of paper. "These are some important numbers," he said. "One is for the state's victim compensation program. They can help with medical bills, therapy, even lost wages. The other is a women's support group. They do incredible work, and they can help you. And your daughters."

I stared at the paper long after he walked away. I hadn't thought about counseling or money or anything beyond getting through the next breath. I was still in survival mode, but a tiny part of me was beginning to stir, wondering if maybe I didn't have to carry this alone, if maybe there was still a way forward.

I called the state aid number right away, and the woman on the line was patient and informative, explaining how to apply for compensation, medical bills, therapy, and loss of income. Just knowing help existed brought a flicker of relief. But when it came to the women's support group, I hesitated. I wasn't ready to talk, to relive any of it, especially not in front of strangers.

It wasn't until about a week later, while I was driving with Kristin and Ashley, that everything had come into focus. We were stopped at a red light when a car pulled up next to us. The man behind the wheel casually glanced over in our direction, probably without a second thought. But Kristin immediately panicked. Her whole body tensed, and she started to breathe rapidly.

"Mom, go! Just go!" she pleaded, her voice full of fear.

Her eyes were wide, her face pale. That's when I realized just how deeply this had affected her, not just me. She wasn't okay. None of us were. And this wasn't going to go away on its own.

I called the women's support group that afternoon.

They scheduled a session for the three of us, but it wasn't what I expected. I had pictured sitting together with a therapist, maybe holding hands, maybe crying, maybe finding some way to make sense of it all as a family. But instead, they separated us. I was placed in a group of women. Kristin and Ashley were taken to a separate group for children.

At first, I wasn't sure it was helping them. They didn't talk about the sessions much afterward. But over time, I noticed a change, especially in Kristin. Her paranoia started to ease. The panicked glances over her shoulder lessened. She was still cautious, still affected, but no longer frozen by fear. I think, in their own quiet way, those sessions gave the girls a safe place to process it all.

Me, on the other hand, I was still holding my secret. The part of the story I couldn't speak aloud. The part that made me feel filthy. Guilty. Broken. Like I somehow brought it on myself.

Then one day, I had a full-blown panic attack. I was out with a friend, driving my car, when something inside me came undone. I couldn't breathe. I couldn't think. I pulled over, jumped out of the car, and collapsed on the side of the road in tears. I told him that I just couldn't get back in. Not that car. Not ever again.

He understood. He drove me home and left his own car with me.

The next day, my brother Jun and his wife Ingrid came over. I didn't even have to explain. They had already heard. They sat with me, listened to what I could say, and then gently offered to help me buy a new car. I couldn't afford a replacement on my own, but they insisted. We traded in my old car and they provided the down payment for something safe and reliable.

It wasn't just a car. It was a fresh start. A small piece of power reclaimed. And though I still couldn't say everything out loud, I knew in those moments I was not alone.

I was on medical leave for six months, and the healing process, both physical and emotional, was grueling. Outwardly, I appeared to be getting better. Even the deep red strangle marks around my neck had begun to fade. The girls seemed to be adjusting as best they could. Ashley, in her sweet attempt to bring light to a dark time, would proudly tell people that her mom had "opened a can of whoop ass." She even asked me if it was okay to say that, and I told her it was. I let her have that little piece of strength, something to cling to.

But what no one could see was the war waging inside me. The guilt was relentless. I couldn't stop blaming myself, not just for what happened to me, but for what my daughters had to witness and endure because of it. I kept thinking I had brought this on myself somehow, that this was punishment for something. I was sorry, so deeply sorry, even if I didn't know what for.

At my doctor's urging, I started therapy and began taking antidepressants. I went every week for two years. I can't say it helped in the way I hoped it would. Most sessions felt like I was talking into the void. I kept waiting for some kind of magic phrase or insight that would lift the weight, but it never came. Instead, we often circled around my relationships, especially the one with my mother. How I always felt like I had done something wrong, that I was in trouble even when I wasn't. That childhood pattern of feeling unworthy, of trying to please, had followed me into adulthood and now into this trauma. It didn't fix things, but it helped me begin to understand them.

When I returned to work, it became an unexpected outlet, a way to reenter the world and focus on something other than the awful secret I had buried deep inside me. Gradually, I began to feel like I was reclaiming pieces of my life.

But the trauma still lived in me. I continued to have nightmares. Sometimes the girls would rush into my room to wake me, only to find my hands wrapped tightly around my own neck in a chokehold, reliving the terror in my sleep. It happened often. For two years, therapy helped me tread water, and eventually the nightmares started to fade. They still show up from time to time but not like before.

I carried that secret for nearly three decades, burying it deep, pretending it didn't shape me. But the shame, guilt, and nightmares lingered. They were heavy, relentless, feeding into years of severe depression. I thought I could rise above it, ignore it, move on, but healing does not work that way. It took a long time to understand that speaking the truth is not weakness. It is power. That night left a mark on my life, but eventually, I reclaimed myself and stepped into the light.

As I sit here now, writing this and reliving the experience, it almost feels like it happened to someone else, as if I were just a spectator watching from a distance. But then the pain rises up again, the images become vivid, and I remember that it was me. I lived through it.

I now understand why so many women never report rape, not to the authorities, not even to the people they love. Shame is a powerful silencer. So is guilt. But here's what I've learned: it wasn't my fault.

I write this now with the hope that anyone reading this who has lived through something similar will understand that they are not alone. Don't suffer in silence. Don't carry the shame that doesn't belong to you. Cry out. Reach out. Because if you don't, you may spend your life fighting a private war with yourself.

And you deserve peace.

You deserve healing.

You deserve to live unafraid.

As far as I know, they never caught him. And sadly, statistics show that most rapists are never brought to justice. That reality and knowing the odds has silenced so many victims, and I now understand why. But I also understand the cost of silence. It's heavy. It's isolating. And it keeps you bound to something that was never yours to carry. While justice may not always come, healing can begin the moment you stop carrying it alone.

Perhaps if I hadn't tried to carry it all by myself, the weight of depression would not have run its course so relentlessly. But memories from my childhood, the familiar feeling that everything was somehow my fault, still surfaced in quiet moments, a reminder that some burdens stick with you. And yet, life has a way of nudging you forward, often through the people you meet along the way.

CHAPTER 20
AILEEN—THE MELTING FACE

Though some wounds never fully fade, life has a way of nudging you forward, often through the people you meet along the way. Aileen was one of those people. She joined FIDM about five years after me, and the moment I met her, her energy was impossible to ignore. To say she was spunky would be an understatement. Aileen was firecracker energy in a five-foot-four-inch frame. She was bold and never hesitated to say what was on her mind, even when it probably would have been wiser not to. There was absolutely nothing meek about her.

We grew closer during our annual end-of-year FIDM trips. Every other year, the destination was Hawaii, where we spent long sun-drenched days lounging on the white sands of Mauna Kea beach, drinks in hand and deadlines far behind us. The in-between years took us to other parts of the world, often Europe, where we explored new cities, got lost in foreign streets, and collected stories we would retell for years. We laughed, we vented, we bonded.

Florence, Italy, had always been my favorite. Florence itself was enchanting with its elegant streets and impeccably dressed locals; even the children seemed to have stepped out of a fashion editorial. The food was unforgettable, the art and architecture overwhelming in the best way, and the city pulsed with a history you could feel in your bones. We stayed at a beautiful hotel in a piazza right in the heart of it all. At night, the square glowed under soft golden lights, and the cathedral looked like something straight out of a dream. Postcard-perfect didn't begin to cover it, because this time, we were living it.

One particular year, Aileen and I decided to extend the magic with our own little European escape after the official FIDM trip wrapped. We had meticulously planned an itinerary, and as always with Aileen, the excitement was infectious.

From Florence, we boarded a train bound for Venice. We spent the entire day wandering through the winding alleys and over the arched bridges of that dreamlike city. Every corner felt like a painting come to life. We browsed quaint little shops, admired the charm of centuries-old buildings, and soaked in the serenity Venice so effortlessly offers.

Before catching our next train, we stopped for dinner at a small trattoria along the Grand Canal. We split a pizza, ordered a carafe of wine, and sat at a table outside, letting the warm breeze kiss our cheeks. It was the kind of evening you try to memorize while you're still living it. The sun dipped low, casting a golden shimmer over the water, and just beyond our table, gondolas floated by with couples leaning into each other as if choreographed by the city itself.

We sat there, tipsy on wine and wanderlust, feeling like we were exactly where we were meant to be. Our laughter blended with the lapping of the water and the soft hum of accordion music somewhere in the distance. What made it even more special was the anticipation, the quiet thrill of knowing this was just the beginning. After Venice, we were off to explore Vienna, Budapest, and Prague. Cities layered in history and culture, each promising its own magic. We couldn’t wait. There’s a rare kind of joy in traveling with someone whose spirit matches your own: spontaneous, curious, and endlessly open to the unknown. That was Aileen.

With full hearts and full bellies, we boarded our train under a moonlit sky. We were two women chasing adventure across Europe, one unforgettable stop at a time.

It was about a twelve-hour train ride from Venice to Vienna. While our compartment was comfortable, sleep was scarce. By the time we arrived, I felt a tickle in my throat; something was definitely brewing. I ignored it. We were running on fumes, checked into our hotel, grabbed a quick dinner, and tried to rest for our early morning castle tour. By evening, the tickle had turned into a full-blown cold, or maybe even the flu. I was a congested, coughing mess.

If anyone was going to rescue me, it was Aileen. We made our way to the small bar in the hotel. She immediately asked the bartender for a hot toddy. When he stared at her blankly, she didn't miss a beat. "Excuse me, I'll show you how to make it," she said, sliding behind the bar like she owned the place.

I sat back in the lobby, miserable, but watching her in action made me laugh out loud.

She emerged proudly with a steaming cup in hand, placed it in front of me, and said, "Drink up. I'll make you another when you're done. Gotta kill all those cooties."

And drink I did. We called it a night early, knowing I needed rest. The next morning, I actually felt better. Way better. That woman knew how to mix a mean hot toddy: equal parts whiskey, lemon, honey, and love.

The next morning, we joined our tour group and met *him*: our tour guide. Young, charming, and gorgeous in that effortlessly European way. Aileen and I, both divorced and single, instantly reverted to giddy schoolgirls. Whenever he glanced our way, we elbowed each other and whispered:

"Did you see him look at me?"

"Please, he was definitely looking at me."

We bickered playfully the entire tour like two teenagers fighting over a celebrity crush. Vienna, with its regal beauty, stately architecture, and grand charm, may not have stolen my heart, but that silly, flirtatious day sure did.

Our train ride from Vienna to Budapest was short, just under three hours, but it didn't mean it was uneventful. Unlike our long-haul journey from Venice, this train didn't have private compartments. It was a standard car with rows of seating, shoulder-to-shoulder with strangers and no room to hide anything.

Somewhere along the route, about an hour outside of Budapest, the train screeched to a stop at a remote station. The doors slid open, and just like a scene from a spy movie, several military officers in dark uniforms stepped aboard. Alongside them was a massive German Shepherd, muscular, focused, and clearly trained to sniff out trouble.

A hush fell over the car. Everyone sat up straighter. Eyes followed the soldiers as they moved with precision down the aisle, the dog weaving between passengers like it had done a hundred times before.

Then I felt Aileen's breath against my ear as she whispered, "I have a joint hidden inside a tampon in the overhead bin."

I whipped my head toward her. "Are you joking?" I mouthed, eyes wide.

She wasn't. Not even close.

My heart plummeted. Panic surged, and every muscle in my body locked up. A joint? On an international train? With armed soldiers and a drug-sniffing dog just a few feet away? Was she out of her mind?

I've never liked marijuana. My first experience in high school was a paranoid nightmare. I thought everyone around me was out to kill me. I tried it a couple more times, hoping it was a fluke. It wasn't. Each time, the same thing: heart racing, mind spiraling, pure terror. That was enough to swear off it for life.

Aileen, on the other hand, found it relaxing, calming even. Normally, I didn't mind that some of my friends smoked. But this? This was something else entirely. Marijuana wasn't legal anywhere in Europe at the time, except in the Netherlands. We were nowhere near the Netherlands. We were headed straight for Budapest.

"What are we going to do?" she hissed, face pale.

"There's nothing we can do," I whispered. "Just act normal."

The soldiers moved methodically, row by row. The dog's nose scanned every inch. Then he reached us. The German Shepherd paused at my feet. My stomach lurched. I braced myself, every horror story I'd ever heard about foreign prisons flashing through my brain. Headlines, prison bars, *Midnight Express*—I could hear metal gates slamming shut.

The dog sniffed, lingered, and then moved on. Just like that, they passed us by.

"Oh my God. Oh my God," we said. "You are never doing that again. Do you hear me?" I hissed. She nodded, eyes still wide with disbelief.

By the time we arrived in Budapest, we were beyond relieved. The city unfolded like a forgotten fairytale. Sweeping Danube, dramatic Parliament, and castles perched high above the city created sensory overload dazzling and unforgettable.

That evening, we dined al fresco under glowing streetlamps, toasting to being alive and not in an international prison. By morning, we were ready to take it all in. Every street corner held centuries of history, every building whispered its own story.

We splurged on a full-day pass at one of Budapest's famed thermal spas, including massages. The entrance alone felt regal. It was part ancient bathhouse, part palace, with echoing domes, intricate tiles, and steam swirling in shafts of sunlight.

We changed into our swimsuits and made our way to the indoor pools. Naked bodies roamed freely as if it were the most normal thing in the world. Aileen and I tried to play it cool, but inside we were like schoolgirls in sex-ed class. Giggles bubbled up every time we turned a corner.

Curious, we stepped into one of the steam capsule saunas, small round pods built to hold six people. At first, the thick mist made it impossible to see anything clearly. We settled onto the benches, thinking we had the space to ourselves. Then, as the steam slowly dissolved, we realized we were not alone. Two fully naked men were sitting there, cool as cucumbers, chatting away in their own language, not a towel in sight.

Aileen and I froze, eyes wide, hearts racing. We glanced at each other, stifling the urge to laugh—or scream. After a few awkward moments, we bolted upright, muttered something that resembled an apology, and shuffled out of the capsule, robes flapping behind us.

The massages that followed were blissful, a true spiritual reset after the chaos, nerves, and hilarity of the day.

Another adventure came when we arrived in Prague. We had been warned about pickpockets, and our nerves were on high alert. When we pulled into the central station just before midnight, it was eerie and dimly lit, almost post-apocalyptic in feeling. There were slumped bodies everywhere, some drunk, some homeless, and the bustle of a normal station was absent.

Our plan was to catch a taxi to our hotel, simple in theory. But neither of us had the local currency, Czech koruna, and the taxi drivers didn't accept credit cards. To make matters worse, the only ATM was downstairs. It was midnight, and the station was eerily quiet, almost empty, except for a few drunks sleeping on the floors. Aileen stayed above with our luggage, determined to guard it like a one-woman battalion. I bolted down the creaky escalator, my heart hammering in my chest. Each click of the keypad felt deafening in the stillness around me as I fumbled for the cash, yanking it out as fast as I could, feeling every eye on me—even if there were barely any people awake to see it.

Once I scrambled back upstairs with the money in hand, we finally secured a taxi and settled into our hotel. The relief of being safely inside allowed us to catch our breath.

The next morning, we woke to the smell of fresh bread and coffee drifting up from the tiny café downstairs in our charming hotel. After breakfast, we spent the day wandering through Prague's cobblestone streets, completely enchanted. Towering spires loomed overhead, intricate carvings adorned every facade, and shadowy alleyways wound like secret passages through the city. It felt like stepping into a gothic fairy tale—or maybe even Gotham City, with its dramatic angles and mysterious energy.

We crossed the iconic Charles Bridge, marveling at the statues that lined its edges, and paused to watch street performers and musicians add life to the centuries-old surroundings. Every corner we turned revealed another breathtaking scene: colorful baroque buildings, hidden courtyards, and ornate gates that looked like they belonged in a movie set. The city felt alive, theatrical, and just a little dangerous in the most thrilling way.

At one point, pausing at the edge of the bridge and taking in the shadowy spires against the overcast sky, I whispered to Aileen, "I feel like Batman's gonna swoop down at any moment."

She grinned without missing a beat. "Not if Dracula gets you first."

We laughed and continued on, ducking into little boutiques, buying trinkets we didn't need, and marveling at the beauty around every corner. Lunch was a quiet affair at a tiny café tucked away in a narrow alley, where we sipped rich coffee and nibbled on pastries, savoring the moment. Prague had an energy that felt as if secrets were tucked around every corner, daring you to discover them. It was thrilling, mysterious, and unlike anywhere else we had ever been.

By the time evening rolled around, we were exhausted but exhilarated, having soaked in all the beauty and mystery Prague had to offer. Little did we know, the day of our departure would bring its own unexpected adventure.

The next morning, we packed our bags and headed to the station to catch our train. Everything seemed straightforward, until it wasn't. As we maneuvered our luggage into our compartment, two sharply dressed young men appeared, offering to help. Something immediately felt off. As I lifted my suitcase, it slipped backward, and I realized one of them was tugging it down. My heart lurched. At that exact moment, the other man disappeared.

Without thinking, I dropped everything and tore into the corridor after him. Thanks to all the 10K races I had run, I was fast, my legs pumping hard. Adrenaline surged through me as I closed the gap. I leapt onto his back, knocking him off balance, and we crashed to the floor in a chaotic tangle. That's when I realized he had been trying to steal my brand-new Bottega Veneta bag. It flew from his hands and skidded across the ground. I grabbed it in a fury and screamed every furious word I could think of as he scrambled up and disappeared.

Back in the compartment, Aileen and a fellow passenger stared at me in disbelief. "Are you okay?" they gasped. I checked my bag, passport, credit cards, cash—all still there. The conductor had seen the men flee but could not do more as the train was ready to depart. Hearts racing, nerves frayed, we finally exhaled.

After a few hours we transferred to our long fifteen-hour overnight train to Milan. This time, we had a private compartment with pull-out bunks, but our nerves were still frayed. Hoping to take the edge off our post-theft trauma, we made our way to the train's bar, and we each had a glass of wine.

Back in our compartment, it quickly became clear that one glass wasn't enough. I convinced Aileen to return to the bar for more. She came back carrying a full bottle, and we poured generously, raising another toast. Feeling the warmth spread through us, we decided to split an Ambien, something I had used before with no issue. But I had never mixed it with wine.

As Aileen talked, her face began to warp, like a movie stuck in slow motion. Her features started to drip downward, like wax sliding off a candle. Her forehead collapsed into deep creases, her eyes stretched, her cheeks drooped, and her mouth sagged into a surreal swirl. I couldn't move or speak. I was mesmerized. What lasted less than a minute felt like hours.

"Don't panic," I said calmly. "Your face is melting."

She burst into laughter. "You're hallucinating! Ambien and alcohol don't always mix!"

Her face slowly fell back into place, the melting, surreal distortion easing until she looked normal again. I was relieved and a little disappointed. It had been oddly mesmerizing.

Sleep finally came, fitful and restless, as the day's chaos replayed in my mind like a thriller. By the time we arrived in Milan, we were completely fried, still laughing at the absurdity of it all.

We stayed one night in Milan before catching our flight home. Exhausted but exhilarated, boarding the plane, we didn't need to say it out loud: this wasn't just a vacation. It was a once-in-a-lifetime journey—full of laughter, fear, adventure, beauty, and sisterhood.

But beneath the lightness of those days, something inside me had begun to awaken. In the years since that night, I had carried a secret I rarely allowed myself to name, burying it so deeply that I tried to believe it no longer had power over me. But buried pain rarely stays buried forever. And somewhere along the way, the weight of everything I had kept hidden began to rise again—quiet at first, then heavier, settling into my thoughts more often than before.

As the plane lifted and Milan faded beneath the clouds, I felt both gratitude for the journey we had shared and a familiar unease stirring within me. I was leaving behind the freedom of those days and returning to a life where the shadows I had long tried to outrun were waiting for me once again.

CHAPTER 21
THE GF CLUB

I had been living in my Moraga condo for two years, but a familiar loneliness lingered. I adored my job at FIDM, yet outside of work, I had no friends and no partner. Ashley was away at college, and Kristin was grown and building her own life. Nights were quiet, too quiet, and the old guilt and sadness I had carried since childhood crept in again.

To ease the loneliness, I got Rupert, my fawn pug, and six months later, Mona, my shiny black one. They brought joy, but I still longed for real connection. So I moved to Danville, imagining a fresh start in a picturesque town full of tree-lined streets and cozy wine bars.

But once I settled into my beautiful new home, the silence returned. My friends lived far, I was not dating, and weekends stretched out painfully empty. After nearly two years of this isolation, I did something bold, maybe even desperate. I posted an ad on Craigslist looking for girlfriends.

The first woman I connected with was a soccer mom. We agreed to meet for coffee and decided to exchange photos beforehand. I sent a picture that I felt captured me, fashionably dressed, smiling warmly, soft makeup, polished hair.

She sent one back along with a note: "This is me. I keep my hair short like Dorothy Hamill because it is easy. No fuss." And she was not kidding. She looked like the archetype of every suburban soccer mom, practical, unpolished, minimal effort.

The morning of our coffee date, I received an email. She was canceling. "I do not think we are compatible," she wrote. A blow-off from a woman. That one stung. I had been rejected by men before, but this felt different.

Like the universe had just said, "Not even for friends." I did not know whether to laugh or cry.

But I did not give up. I browsed other ads and found one from a woman named Cherie. From our first messages, it just worked. We loved the same things and even had birthdays a day apart. We met at a wine bar in Danville and clicked instantly. Conversation flowed easily. We laughed at the same things and even ordered the same wine without realizing it.

As the night wore on, Cherie and I were fully in our element, sipping wine, enjoying the soft pulse of live jazz drifting through the room, and talking about music. The conversation turned to Latin jazz, and somehow we ended up raving about Pete Escovedo, the legendary percussionist and father of Sheila E. We both adored his music.

I kid you not, what happened next felt like something out of a movie. Just as we looked up from our glasses mid-conversation, we saw *him* walk into the wine bar. Pete Escovedo in the flesh. He strolled in with two other men and passed right by us at the bar. Cherie and I were frozen. He must have noticed us gawking because he gave a warm "Good evening" as he walked past.

We blurted out that we had just been talking about him. Pete grinned and said, "I hope you were saying good things." Then they moved to a high-top table nearby.

Before we could even recover, one of his companions walked over. He introduced himself as Victor and said they would love for us to join them. Pete would be honored, he said.

Yes. No thinking needed. We grabbed our glasses and joined them.

The other man introduced himself as Joey. He often played at the same wine bar, though tonight he was there to enjoy the music. Pete mentioned Joey was also his bodyguard. Joey laughed, but none of us doubted he could handle it.

We slipped into an easy rhythm of conversation. Pete was charming, down-to-earth, and full of stories. He lived in Los Angeles but was originally from the East Bay and visited often. Victor and Joey were locals.

Before the night ended, Victor told us Pete had a performance in San Francisco in a couple of weeks. He handed me his number and said, "If you decide to go, call me. I will get you and your friends tickets and make sure we come out to say hello."

We were definitely going.

The night of the concert was magical. Our group was mid-conversation at dinner when Pete and Victor walked over to our table. They greeted Cherie and me personally and then introduced themselves to everyone. Pete even stayed a few minutes before heading backstage.

Our seats were excellent, courtesy of Victor. A few minutes later, he came back with another woman and brought her to the empty seat right next to mine. He smiled and said, "Everyone, this is Judi. She is here alone tonight and lives near you, Janette."

From the moment she sat down, I noticed her warmth. Judi smiled easily. It was natural for her. As I sat next to her, I suddenly felt self-conscious. I thought of all the times in my life when people would tell me to smile, as if it were effortless. They never understood that it was not. After everything I had been through, a smile did not always come naturally. At work, I could turn it on, but in my personal life, it was not automatic. Not until now—now that things were slowly changing. Judi was personable and thoughtful, and we shared many interests. We clicked, and that was just the beginning.

Around the same time, I had been chatting online with another woman named Laura, an attorney who, like me, wanted to connect with other women. She suggested a group meet-up, and several of us agreed.

We met one Saturday afternoon at a Starbucks in Walnut Creek. There were six to eight of us. Laura was tall, blonde, and stylish. I also met Yolanda that day, stunning with high cheekbones and a radiant smile. It was hard to get to know everyone in a group setting, but we exchanged numbers and planned to meet again.

Laura and I kept in touch and decided our next meet-up should be a wine bar in Danville. I invited the Starbucks group, plus Cherie and Judi.

That night, Laura, Yolanda, a couple of others, Cherie, and Judi all showed up. The vibe was relaxed, the wine flowing, and the conversations deepened. Something was forming.

More outings followed. Movies, outdoor concerts, art and wine festivals, coffee dates. Yolanda brought in more women, and soon our circle grew.

Eventually, we started calling ourselves The GF Club, short for Girlfriend Club. A light-hearted name for something truly special.

Laura and I grew very close. Maybe because neither of us were dating at the time, or maybe because some friendships simply fall into place. Later that year, I invited her to be my guest on FIDM's end-of-year trip to Hawaii. She said yes, and we spent a week at the Mauna Kea Beach Resort. Sun-soaked days, ocean breezes, endless laughter. That trip cemented our bond.

From then on, we called each other SS, short for Soul Sister. We traveled together often, including a fantastic trip to New York. One year, we went even bigger and took a Western Mediterranean cruise out of Barcelona. We shopped like it was an Olympic sport and somehow got everything home without extra luggage fees.

Life kept evolving. Laura fell in love with a man, and I started dating Ron. He was divorced and said it ended because his ex-wife had cheated.

One night, some of the GF girls and I were at a wine bar in Danville, and Ron joined us. While I waited alone at the bar for our drinks, a woman approached. She asked, "Is his name Ron?"

My stomach tightened. What now?

She introduced herself as Irma and said, "I think his ex-wife had an affair with my ex-husband." It sounded like a soap opera. Their exes had worked at the same company. Their affair ended both marriages.

Ron spoke with her, and afterward Irma joined us. I introduced her to the GF girls, and just like that, she became one of us.

Later that year, right before the holidays, Ron intercepted a party invitation meant for his ex-wife. It was for Gordon Getty's seventy-sixth birthday gala. Heavy cream cardstock, elegant calligraphy, embossed gold. It whispered wealth.

Ron asked if I wanted to go.

"Are you kidding? Yes."

I called Irma. She had intercepted the same invitation, intended for her ex. Their company had done business with the Gettys. A lucky mistake in our favor.

Ron booked us a hotel in San Francisco. I wore a black Marc Jacobs cocktail dress. Ron wore a tailored black suit. It was pouring rain, but nothing dimmed the excitement. When we arrived at the Getty mansion in Pacific Heights, staff with massive umbrellas ushered us inside.

The most lavish oyster bar I had ever seen stretched before us. Room after room had themed food stations. My favorite was the cheese room, overflowing with cheeses from all over the world. Ron loved the carving station. Champagne flowed freely.

I saw former Mayor Willie Brown and introduced myself. Later, I met Mayor Gavin Newsom and his wife. He was incredibly handsome. We took a photo with him standing between us, and I will admit that his wife did not make it into my final cropped version.

In one room, people danced under crystal chandeliers. In another, a group of men in tuxedos stood together like an exclusive club. I snapped photos. Ann Getty herself stopped to greet me warmly.

Then I saw Irma, stunning in a red satin gown. She had brought her friend Leslie. We mingled, drank champagne, and soaked up the surreal atmosphere.

Sixteen years later, while flipping through pictures from that night, I saw someone familiar. One of the tuxedoed men in that private corner was Jeffrey Epstein. Chills ran through me. I remembered his smug expression. It felt eerie in hindsight.

That night was unforgettable. A total fluke. Technically we were party crashers, but I have no regrets. Sometimes life hands you an invitation you were not supposed to receive, and you RSVP yes anyway.

Looking back, it is hard to believe that a simple Craigslist post, born out of loneliness and a longing for connection, would open the door to some of the deepest, most meaningful friendships of my life. Weekend wine bar meetups turned into soul-deep sisterhoods, full of laughter, adventure, and unwavering support. These women came into my life when I did not even realize how much I needed them. We found each other in the most unexpected ways, yet somehow it all felt meant to be. Somewhere along the way, the loneliness lifted. I had my tribe, my girlfriends, my chosen family.

But even surrounded by love, something inside me was still unsettled. The guilt, the shadows, the quiet ache I had carried for years did not disappear just because I finally had people beside me. The friendships filled my days with joy and adventure, but they could not silence the deeper pain that lived beneath the surface. I did not know it yet, but friendship alone would not be enough to lift me out of the depression that still lingered. That part of my healing was still waiting for me.

CHAPTER 22
BIRTHDAY SOIREE

About two years before my fiftieth birthday, I made a bold decision. I was going to throw myself the kind of party people talked about for years. Not a simple dinner with friends or a backyard BBQ. This would be elegant, outrageous, and fabulously over the top. The kind of celebration most people reserved for weddings. Only this one would be for me.

Every payday, I quietly tucked away part of my earnings into a savings account labeled "Fifty and Fabulous." I was determined to pay cash for every detail. I wanted no guilt and no debt. Just pure, joyful indulgence. This wasn't only a party. It was a declaration.

When I got married years earlier, we didn't have a big wedding. It was intimate and beautiful, held at my in-laws' home, but it wasn't the fairy-tale event many girls dream of. For years, I held onto the idea that if I ever remarried, I would finally get that big celebration. But two decades had passed since my divorce, and with time I became more comfortable with the idea that maybe that kind of love story simply wasn't meant for me. And that was more than okay. I did not need a groom or a gown to justify creating an unforgettable moment for myself.

Besides, people spent a fortune on weddings only to end up divorced. No regrets. No heartbreak. Just a woman choosing to celebrate her life. And doing it in style.

As my savings grew, so did the dream. It was no longer a fantasy. It was happening. So I began scouting venues.

After visiting several options, I found the perfect one practically in my own backyard. The Blackhawk Car Museum in Danville. It was stunning with a sleek, spacious gallery filled with rare and classic automobiles that gleamed like polished jewels. The event space had cars displayed right inside the room, giving the setting a vintage glamour that felt extravagant and cool. I knew instantly that the women would be dazzled and the men would be impressed. Perfect.

I booked it and the real work began.

Planning an extravagant party that felt like a mix between a black-tie gala and a fantasy wedding reception was no small task. I quickly understood why people hired event planners. But I had decided to do everything myself. Call it pride or the thrill of complete creative control. Either way, I became a one-woman planning committee.

There were menus to choose, floral arrangements to design, table settings to visualize, and endless decisions about music and lighting. Every detail mattered. I wanted guests to walk in and feel transported.

Even with the occasional overwhelm and more than a few sleepless nights spent mentally rearranging everything, it all began to fall into place. The vision in my mind was becoming real. Elegant. Fun. A little flashy. Completely me.

One of the hardest tasks was creating the guest list. I had to limit it to two hundred guests. For most people, that might seem enormous, but for me and my family, it felt tight. Between friends, relatives, coworkers, and people I had collected through various chapters of my life, narrowing it down felt like trimming a tree with a nail file. I agonized over every name I removed.

Still, getting that list right was a priority. The party was set for May, and I wanted those save-the-date cards out immediately. No way was I going to put all this effort into the celebration of the decade and then have people miss it because they booked a cruise or a graduation party.

The museum recommended an event design company known for transforming spaces into something magical, and they were exceptional. The owner was poised, creative, and full of dramatic flair. Planning with her felt like preparing for a dream wedding. Except the bride was me, and I was marrying life itself. We settled on a yellow-and-black color palette that was bold, joyful, and sophisticated.

When the night of the party arrived, everything shimmered with excitement. A cascading trail of yellow and black balloons lined the grand staircase leading to the open-air foyer, where pre-dinner cocktails were served. I chose an open bar and made a silent agreement with the bartender that he would discreetly let me know if things began getting too festive.

The entrance to the main hall featured a magnificent balloon arch. Inside, guests walked into a breathtaking scene. Classic cars gleamed under soft lights, adding vintage elegance and creating perfect photo opportunities. I hired a live band with incredible energy that had people on their feet within minutes. Fresh flowers added pops of yellow against crisp white tablecloths, and twenty beautifully set tables surrounded the stage and dance floor. Behind the band, a custom gold-script sign read "Happy Birthday Janette," giving the entire room a glamorous, cinematic quality.

And yes, it looked like a wedding. Only this time, the celebration was about honoring myself. I did bring a date, Steve, someone I had just started seeing, although I nearly uninvited him. That is a story for another chapter.

Dinner was elegant, with a choice of prime rib, chicken, or a vegetarian entrée. Prime rib, of course, was the crowd favorite.

The guest list was a tapestry of my life. My immediate family was there, including my mother, who was thankfully still alive to share this milestone with me. Relatives, longtime coworkers, and girlfriends I had grown close to over the past year filled the room with laughter and love. Guests had come from out of town, and several old classmates I had reconnected with through Facebook joined as well, including Rosanne and Arlene from my cheerleading days. My ex-husband Manny was there with his wife, Agnes, as we have remained close over the years and always will. Manny's extended family filled about twenty-five seats, and they had always been family to me, a bond that would never change.

Everyone showed up dressed to impress. The women were elegant in cocktail dresses and glittering gowns. The men wore dark suits and even tuxedos. It felt like a red-carpet evening. Everywhere I looked, there was beauty, style, and celebration. My heart overflowed.

The highlight of the night was my special guest, Pete Escovedo. He had flown in from Los Angeles just for the event. Since we first met at the wine bar in Danville a year earlier, I had slowly developed a friendship with him, his manager Victor, and his close friend Joey. Whenever Pete performed nearby, Victor always saved a booth for me and my friends. That night, the band invited Pete to join them for "Oye Como Va," and the entire room came alive. The dance floor flooded with people, laughter, and electric energy.

The food, drinks, music, and cake were all incredible. The dance floor stayed full all night. Everyone had a wonderful time, especially me. It truly was the party of a lifetime, not only for me but for many of the guests who still talk about it today. The celebration took place fifteen years ago, yet it still feels vivid.

Whenever I look at the photos or watch the beautifully edited video, I get emotional. It was a gift to be surrounded by so many people I loved. But now, when I revisit those memories, a soft sadness settles in. Many of those beloved faces are gone, including my mother. That brings tears, but it also makes me treasure that magical night even more.

Turning fifty was a milestone worth honoring, not because of the number, but because of who I had become. Independent. Resilient. Joyful. I did not have a groom that night, but I had everything else. Family, friends, laughter, love, and a heart full of gratitude. In many ways, it truly was a wedding. One where I married the most important person in my life. Myself.

But even in the glow of that night, something inside me had already begun to unravel. A heaviness I could not name yet. I was celebrating myself, unaware that a new wave of darkness and depression was quietly making its way toward me.

CHAPTER 23
STEVE—THE CONTROL FACTOR

I was dating Steve just before my big birthday soiree. Tall, handsome, and a dead ringer for Liam Neeson, he was a retired policeman, old-school conservative, and had a strong aversion to anything risqué or liberal. Everything about him seemed opposite of me, yet somehow, he reeled me in.

We had only been together for three months when my fiftieth birthday party arrived, yet Steve behaved as if we were already cemented together. He was fourteen years older and a full-blown germophobe who carried sanitizing wipes like sacred objects. He went so far as to call the city of Livermore a "contamination zone," all because of the Lawrence Livermore Lab. When he learned one of my guests worked there, he became almost demanding, insisting I uninvite them, repeating it as if it were a reasonable request.

I finally told him, "If anyone gets uninvited, it will be you." That shut him up for a moment.

He replied in this self-important tone, "Fine, your guest can go, but do not expect me to shake hands with them." He said it as if the party belonged to him. Huge red flag that I ignored.

At the party, he kept it together until I started circulating and greeting guests. He grew visibly irritated, sulking whenever I was not glued to his side. When some friends mentioned an after-party, he cut them off sharply and announced that I was tired and he was taking me home. Something inside me flinched. That should have been another warning I listened to.

When I asked about his daughter, Lisa, he shrugged and said they weren't very close, even making a few jokes at her expense about her interest in psychic work and mystical New Age practices. It wasn't her hobbies that unsettled me, it was how dismissive he was of his own daughter. I've always been close to my kids, no matter their passions, so his attitude toward Lisa made me sad and wary.

We all eventually went out to dinner. I wanted to meet Lisa and her husband, Ken, especially since Steve had mentioned he was a huge San Francisco Giants fan, just like me. Lisa and Ken were both middle-aged, probably closer to my age than to the age gap between Steve and me, which made the dynamic even more interesting.

The night we met, I was instantly charmed. Lisa was stunning with expressive eyes, and Ken was a towering gentle giant, six feet and six inches of pure sweetness. Ken and I hit it off immediately over our shared love of Bay Area sports. Being a season ticket holder, I promised to take him to a Giants game, and one game turned into a few, eventually becoming a full-blown tradition spanning several seasons. We had an absolute blast.

Somewhere along the way, I started calling him "Sonny Boy," and he affectionately began calling me "Mom." We must have been quite the sight, a towering young white guy and a petite Asian woman, publicly calling each other "Mom" and "Son." It never failed to crack us up, and it always left people around us curious about the story behind it.

Meanwhile, my relationship with Steve fell into a predictable rhythm. Dinner at one of the three restaurants he approved of, then back to my place for old black-and-white TV shows. He tolerated some modern shows, but nothing I enjoyed. No movies, no live shows, no spontaneous trips, no adventures outside his comfort zone. The same routine repeated week after week until it felt suffocating.

So when two years passed and the routine never wavered, it made sense that the next step would feel just as controlled. Somehow, by this point, he had already convinced me that at our age, we were fortunate to have found each other, maybe because I had already weathered a number of failed relationships. Or maybe, after everything I had been through, I had stopped believing there was something better meant for me.

He proposed in his own strange way. We were in Monterey at the Best Western Inn, one of the two getaways we occasionally took together. The other was Santa Cruz. After a little wine and ocean breeze, he pulled out a gorgeous diamond ring. He said we did not actually have to get married. He just preferred we call each other "fiancés" instead of boyfriend and girlfriend. No real pressure, no timeline. Somehow, I said yes. Not because I believed in a future with him, but because I believed I could adapt to the parts of him I did not like.

That decision, however, did not change the reality of who he was. He hated my work trips to Los Angeles and resented my personal travel even more. Pole fitness classes, Wine Wednesdays, family time, everything outside of him felt off-limits. I gave in to his rules sometimes, but I drew the line at the parts of my life that mattered most to me.

Even though I held my ground on the parts of my life I valued most, his need to control everything around him was always simmering beneath the surface. That tension became impossible to ignore when I told him I wouldn't be free one weekend. I'd promised to watch my nephews while my sister and her husband went out of town. The boys were staying with me, and I was genuinely looking forward to it. He did not take it well.

"Why do you have to take care of them?" he snapped, like I'd announced I was joining a cult. "Why don't they ask their neighbors or something?"

Excuse me, what?

I tried to explain calmly that spending time with my nephews was something I looked forward to. He wasn't having it. He sulked, ranted, and made it clear that his time came before anyone else's.

We went back and forth, me stunned by his selfishness, him incredulous that I wouldn't put him first over my family for the weekend.

That weekend was the first time I truly stood firm. I told him I wasn't going to let my sister down, and I didn't. I spent the weekend with my nephews and had an absolute blast.

But something had erupted. That incident revealed a part of Steve I couldn't ignore: his controlling tone, lack of empathy, and the belief that his needs always came first. It was no longer a red flag, it was a giant, blinding warning sign.

Yet I didn't act on it. Looking back, I can see how my boundaries slowly eroded, one red flag at a time. And so we returned to our routines: the same tired restaurants, the same old TV shows, the same weekends, like clockwork.

Five years into our relationship, it all came crashing down during dinner one night at Chow, one of our usual restaurants. I mentioned I was stressed from work. Instead of offering support, Steve blamed my stress on everything he disapproved of: my travel, pole dancing, and time with friends. Something inside me broke.

"No," I said louder than I meant to. "You are why I'm stressed."

Years of frustration poured out of me. I told him I felt like I was always tiptoeing around him, like I couldn't breathe unless everything was done his way, like he didn't actually see me. When we got home, I took off the ring and told him it was over. He smiled condescendingly and said I'd feel differently tomorrow, insisting I didn't mean it. He refused to take the ring, so I left it on the kitchen counter.

The next day, I came home from pole fitness, and when I walked in, I froze. He was inside my house. That's when I realized he still had the code to my door. Instead of apologizing, he launched into a lecture about me being unstable and overwhelmed, insisting he was there to help me through it. It was classic gaslighting, rewriting my reality as if I weren't even there.

I stayed calm. I told him clearly that it was over, that I had worn that ring for three years too long, and that nothing he said would change my mind. For the first time, he stopped arguing. He stood up, waved goodbye to Rupert and Mona, and walked out. The ring was still on the counter.

As the door closed behind him, I didn't cry. I felt free. Finally free. I realized then that love is not meant to shrink you or dim you. For too long,

I had made myself smaller just to keep the peace. Ending the relationship should have felt like a clean break.

But freedom didn't erase the shadows I'd carried for years. The creeping depression I'd tried to ignore, the belief that being in a loving relationship wasn't in the cards for me, the fear that maybe this was all I deserved—they all came rushing back. Even in that moment of relief, I could feel them settling around me, a reminder that breaking free was only the beginning, not the end.

CHAPTER 24
TWIRLY GIRLS

The Beginning

Still, life had a way of nudging me forward. Shortly after my fifty-third birthday, I had stumbled upon a Groupon for something I never imagined I would try: a pole fitness class. Pole fitness? At my age? I was intrigued, a little skeptical, but mostly curious. For fifteen dollars, I figured, why not? I immediately called my SS, Laura.

"You have to come with me," I told her. "We will laugh our asses off if nothing else."

She was in. We booked a private session for just the two of us.

The studio was called Twirly Girls, which instantly made me smile. It was cute, catchy, and just cheeky enough to make me hope we were not about to embarrass ourselves permanently.

On the day of our private class, we walked into the studio with nervous energy buzzing between us. The space surprised me. High industrial ceilings, glossy hardwood floors, and silver poles rising like metallic trees. We looked at each other and burst into laughter. What had we signed up for?

Our instructor greeted us warmly and started us off with a basic warm-up, perfectly normal. Then she guided us toward the poles, which she called our dance partners. We learned how to walk around the pole, how to ease into gentle spins, how to let movement replace stiffness. And then came the floorwork.

She lowered herself gracefully, her body melting into the floor like liquid silk. Every slow, deliberate glide was hypnotic, elegant, sensual, and controlled. She moved like a woman who knew exactly who she was in her skin, gliding across the floor with the effortless confidence of a snake. Laura and I sat frozen, wide-eyed, our jaws practically on the floor.

This was not the raunchy spectacle we secretly expected. It was not something to giggle at or dismiss. What we were watching was art. Raw, sensual, powerful, feminine, deeply expressive. Nothing vulgar. Nothing cheap. It was poetry told through muscle and breath. Our assumptions crumbled, replaced with curiosity, admiration, and maybe even a little longing to move like that ourselves.

We gave it our best shot, crawling and stretching like two confused house cats trying to be sultry. We kept catching glimpses of each other in the mirror and dissolving into giggles that echoed through the room. But somewhere between the awkward crawling and shaky spins, something clicked.

Not in the sense that we magically knew what we were doing, but in the sense that we loosened. The laughter felt freer. I stopped worrying about how ridiculous I looked or whether my stomach stuck out or if I was doing anything correctly. Letting go of years of self-consciousness felt rebellious and exhilarating.

I felt aware of my body in a new way, not as something to hide or fix, but as something powerful and alive. My legs felt stronger. My hips remembered they could sway. My hands became expressive. For the first time in years, I felt sexy, not for anyone else, but for myself. It was as though I had uncovered a part of me that had been waiting patiently for permission to wake up.

After that one-hour teaser, I was hooked.

Laura and I high-fived on the way out.

"That was insane," she said, grinning.

"I am signing up for another class," I said before we even got in the car.

Finding My Place

The next day, still buzzing, I left a voicemail for the studio owner. She called me back shortly after. Her name was Bel, but everyone called her Mama Bel. Even her voice felt warm and grounding, like reconnecting with someone I hadn't realized I'd been missing.

She suggested her Friday morning class, assuring me the pace would be perfect. I did not work Fridays, so it felt like fate opening a door.

Meeting Bel in person sealed the deal. She was a petite powerhouse, about my age, with gorgeous, tousled hair and a laugh that could brighten an entire building. Always giggling, always glowing. I adored her instantly.

From the very first class, I was in love. Not just with Bel, but with the vibe. The pulsing music, the dim lights, the laughter bouncing off mirrored walls, the women unapologetically owning their space. No judgment. No competition. No sucking in your stomach or pretending your hips behaved. It felt like finding a secret club where the only rule was to show up and move.

Bel had this effortless magnetism that made you want to try harder without ever feeling inadequate. She treated every woman, from beginners clinging to the pole like a life raft to seasoned dancers spinning upside down in glitter, as if she was part of something magical. I was drawn to her like a moth to flame, and honestly, I would have followed her anywhere, even if it meant crawling seductively across the floor at ten in the morning in front of strangers.

The biggest surprise was the other students I met in this class. I expected twenty-somethings performing acrobatics while the rest of us hid in the back. Not even close. Most of the women were around my age, fifties and fabulous. Women with laugh lines and stories. Women reclaiming their bodies, their sensuality, their joy. There was sass, sisterhood, and laughter that made your abs hurt more than any workout.

Bel took me under her wing. She guided me toward classes that fit my level, gave gentle tips, and celebrated every small win. Before long, I was there three times a week, chasing the high of movement, laughter, and belonging. Outside the studio, we bonded even more. Dinners, drinks, long talks. She became more than a teacher. She became a real friend, a confidante, a spark.

This place, these people, this wild pole adventure awakened something in me. A part of myself I did not realize had gone quiet.

Let me be clear: I am not a dancer. Oh, I love dancing, but being good at it? Not even close. Rhythm and I have always had a toxic relationship. I chased it; it ghosted me. I'm pretty sure I'm tone-deaf. I cannot carry a tune, I cannot follow a beat, and I've spent more time tripping over my own feet than gliding anywhere gracefully.

But none of that ever stopped me. I've had a passion for dance my entire life. Even knowing I was always off-beat, always slightly off-rhythm, I kept moving anyway. Dancing made me feel alive. It reminded me that joy wasn't about perfection, it was about showing up, letting go, and giving myself permission to move through life on my own terms.

But in Bel's studio, none of that mattered. Perfection was not the goal. Presence was. She focused on safety, strength, awareness, and joy. She made every woman feel welcome, no matter how wobbly her spins were or how confused her arms became.

Her one non-negotiable was this: "Point your damn toes."

I can still hear her yelling it across the room. No matter what move you attempted, graceful or awkward, those toes had to be pointed. If they were not, she scolded us mercilessly, calling them "monkey feet." I would be flailing like a wind-up toy, giving it everything I had, and she would clap her hands, eyes blazing, and say, "Great effort. Now point your damn toes."

It cracked me up every time. But she taught us something deeper. Movement did not have to be perfect to be powerful. Beauty could be messy, sweaty, bruised. Grace was not precision. Grace was presence.

Friday mornings quickly became my favorite time of the week. That is where I met Sylvia and Brenda, both around my age. We bonded immediately over bruised knees, sweaty laughs, and post-class coffee dates that grew into real friendship.

Pole fitness was not just a new hobby. It was a portal to a bolder, freer, more connected version of myself.

The Spotlight

About a year in, Bel dropped a bomb. "You should be in the recital."

I laughed so hard I almost pulled a muscle. Absolutely not. I had two left feet and zero confidence. But Bel had a way of making her students feel worthy of a spotlight. When I hesitated, she added, "It is a fundraiser for the Kidney Foundation. It is called Lovely Rita, in honor of Rita, one of our students who has undergone multiple kidney transplants."

That changed everything.

I knew Rita. Soft-spoken, radiant, quietly strong. If she could survive everything she had endured, I could survive five minutes on a stage.

So with Bel's belief louder than my fear, I shocked myself by saying yes.

To prepare, I started working one-on-one with AJ, one of the male instructors. Watching him dance was like watching water move. Graceful, effortless, mesmerizing. Flirty, fierce, fabulous. He was born for a spotlight.

At first, I was intimidated. How was I supposed to keep up with that? But once we started training, the nerves faded. AJ's belief in me was genuine. He never made me feel silly. He would grin and say, "You got this, girl," and somehow I believed him.

And then he taught me something I still hear in my head to this day: "Look at the audience. Connect with them. Let them feel you."

We picked the perfect song: "Big Spender." Bold, cheeky, theatrical. AJ built a sassy, Broadway-style routine with every wink, hip roll, and hair flip perfectly placed. We rehearsed for weeks, laughing, sweating, falling, trying again. He added a twist: fake money I would toss into the audience at the end. Outrageous. Fabulous. Perfect.

But as show night approached, old nerves started to creep in.

The evening of the show, a memory hit me so hard it felt physical.

Suddenly I was fourteen again, standing onstage at my junior high school cheerleading tryout. Wearing a frumpy outfit, fumbling every move, feeling the sting of whispered laughter from the girls watching. I knew I did not belong. I knew I failed. That humiliation had buried itself deep, deeper than I realized.

It still had claws in me.

And now, all these years later, those same old feelings crept back. Doubt. Shame. Not-enoughness. They came roaring in so fiercely that I almost backed out. I really did. I told myself I was too old, too off-beat, too "what-was-I-thinking" to pull this off. The insecure teenager inside me was begging me to sit down and stay small.

But then I thought of Bel. And AJ. And my fellow Twirly Girls cheering me on. I thought about the strength I had worked so hard to reclaim. And I thought about that stage waiting for me. I took a breath, pointed my toes, and decided I wasn't letting that old story win.

I stepped out under the lights, momentarily blinded but buzzing with adrenaline. The opening notes of "Big Spender" filled the room, bold and brassy. The crowd clapped along, and some even chanted my name. My name. That alone nearly made my knees buckle.

But I didn't freeze. I smiled, and I gave it attitude. I swayed my hips, slow and deliberate, syncing my breath with the beat. My movements had intention, a little extra snap in the turns, a little smirk in the sway. The nerves dissolved into the rhythm. Each move was rehearsed, yes, but in that moment I was dancing from instinct, not memory.

I wrapped my hand around the cool metal of the pole and let myself spin, hair flipping, body gliding, heels clicking in time. I wasn't just hitting the marks. I was performing. Commanding. Owning every second of it.

Then came my favorite move, the one I had worked so hard to master. I climbed. One grip, then another. My thighs tightened around the pole as I pulled myself upward, muscle by trembling muscle. I reached the top, held for a beat, and then dropped in a dramatic, controlled slide that ended in a perfect, cheeky landing. The crowd erupted. The sound hit me like a wave.

With a wink, I tossed a handful of play money into the audience and strutted to the next pole, spinning around it with flair before throwing out another handful of bills. I was working the stage like a seasoned showgirl. Finally, I returned to the front pole, spun one last time, struck a pose, and took a bow like I owned the place. And for that moment, I did.

For the first time in my life, I wasn't just surviving a performance. I was owning it. I wasn't the awkward girl trying to keep up or the woman terrified of looking foolish. I was a star. Strong. Sexy. Shamelessly alive. I had climbed that pole, and metaphorically, I had climbed out of every box I had ever been put in.

As I stepped off the stage, cheeks flushed, legs shaking, hearing my fellow Twirly Girls cheering their hearts out, one thought hit me. *Damn. I did that.*

From Passion to Purpose

After that first performance, I returned to the stage for several more Lovely Rita recitals. No, I never became the most technical or graceful dancer, but something far more powerful happened. I learned to feel at home in my own skin. I moved with confidence, not perfection. And I owed so much of that to the steady encouragement of Bel and AJ. They didn't just teach pole. They helped me rediscover myself.

Somewhere in the middle of this newfound passion, I began chatting with a man I met online. His name was Donny, and although he lived on the East Coast, our conversations had an unexpected spark. He owned a public relations company and had a mile-a-minute brain full of quirky, off-the-wall, oddly brilliant ideas. When I told him about my pole fitness journey, he immediately said, "You need a Facebook page for that. People would love this."

I laughed it off, but then he said something that stopped me cold. "Why don't you start your own pole fitness clothing line?"

Wait. What?

I wasn't a designer. I couldn't even sew a button without cursing, but the idea lit me up. I brought it to Bel the next day, fully expecting her to laugh.

Instead, her eyes widened and she clapped her hands. "Yes. Do it. That is so you," she said. "And make sure your clothes feel fierce, fun, and unapologetically badass."

With her encouragement and Donny's relentless enthusiasm, I dove in. I wasn't sketching patterns or sewing fabrics. I was sourcing stylish, ready-made pieces and giving them my own bold, empowering twist. And that is how Live For Pole was born.

I filed for a business license, opened an online shop, and got to work. Soon I was stocking everything: tee shirts, hoodies, joggers, tanks, hats, bags, all stamped with phrases like "I'm a Pole Dancer!" and "Live For Pole."

What started as a side hustle turned into a full-blown passion project. It wasn't just about selling clothes. It was about claiming space, celebrating confidence, and giving women a nudge to embrace their power, one sassy crop top at a time.

Donny wasn't kidding about growing the Facebook page. I named it "I'm a Pole Dancer," bold and proud. The numbers climbed fast. What started as a small community exploded into a global one. Before long, there were nearly twenty thousand members from around the world. I loved seeing their photos, their progress, their joy. These weren't just dancers. They were athletes and artists.

To honor the talent in the group, I started choosing one pole dancer each month to feature as the page's cover photo. They would send stunning images that captured strength and grace, and I posted them proudly. They often thanked me, saying what an honor it was. But the honor was mine.

About a year later, after my online shop gained momentum, I made a bold leap and bought a vendor booth for Live For Pole at Pole Expo at the Hard Rock Hotel in Las Vegas. I had attended the year before with some Twirly Girls, and the energy was unforgettable. Vendor halls buzzing with music, glitter, performances, and laughter. I had walked through those halls thinking, *Someday I'll be back… behind one of these tables.*

And I was. The next year, I stood behind my own booth, positioned perfectly across from the stage. People passed by all day, stopping to watch performers, then wandering over to my merchandise. It felt surreal.

That is also when I met Fawnia, the woman behind Pole Expo. She was legendary, known as the first legitimate pole fitness instructor in the United States. And she was beautiful, the kind of pretty that turned heads, but with a presence that made her beauty feel effortless. Despite the thousands of attendees, she made a point to come welcome me personally. She wasn't a diva or an untouchable icon. She was warm, grounded, kind, and just as stunning inside as she was on the outside.

Standing there with my own brand, surrounded by the community that had inspired me from the beginning, I realized how far I had come from that first Groupon class with Laura. I was no longer just trying pole dancing. I was living it.

For the next few years, I returned to Pole Expo with pride, setting up my booth year after year. I also traveled to the East Coast for Pole Con and other conventions, immersing myself even deeper into the glittering world of pole fitness. But Pole Expo was always home. And Fawnia became more than the founder. She became a friend.

In 2016, I made another bold move when I relocated to Las Vegas. Suddenly, Pole Expo was in my backyard. But that story is for another chapter.

Through all those years of recitals, vendor booths, sequins, sweat, and spinning poles, I discovered something far more powerful than the physical workout. I found connection. I met women and men from every walk of life, of all ages and stories. Some of them became lifelong friends. Bel eventually sold Twirly Girls, but we still stay in touch. That bond we built through bruises, laughter, and endless practice never faded.

No, I never became a pole dance prodigy. I still lack rhythm, and I am perfectly fine with that. Because what I gained was confidence, joy, and community. The lonely, self-conscious girl who once thought she didn't belong anywhere finally found her place. I went from feeling invisible to feeling seen, celebrated, and connected with people all over the world who taught me that strength comes in many forms, and beauty is never defined by perfection.

Pole fitness didn't just change my body. It changed my life.

CHAPTER 25
FAREWELL FIDM

By early 2016, I was running on fumes. The daily commute from Danville to San Francisco, which once took a manageable forty-five minutes, had turned into a soul-crushing hour and a half, sometimes two. Traffic had gotten so bad it felt like the Bay Area was conspiring to break me down one mile at a time.

Public transportation wasn't an option, not with my late-night hours and certainly not after my second kidnapping on BART. I avoided the train completely after that. No convenience was worth that kind of fear.

Meanwhile, everything else kept climbing: property taxes, gas, groceries, you name it. The cost of living wasn't just high; it was punishing. I felt squeezed from all sides. Friends gently suggested I consider leaving California, but most of my family was still in the Bay Area, except for Ashley in San Diego. Leaving entirely didn't feel right. Not yet.

Eventually I faced the truth. I would sell my house, pocket whatever profit I could, and figure out the rest later. But the moment I thought that, another question rose up like a stubborn shadow. Did I really want to leave FIDM?

I had been there thirty years, longer than many marriages last. It had become part of my identity. I weighed the stability against the stress, the memories against the mounting bills, and finally admitted the truth I had been avoiding. Staying didn't make sense anymore.

So I gave my notice.

Before telling my director, I pulled Aileen and a few close friends aside. We cried, hugged, and reminisced. Then I walked into my director's office and broke the news. It was emotional, but everyone understood. With the way things were going in the Bay Area, I wasn't the only one being priced out of my life.

Once the decision was made, everything moved fast. I listed my house, expecting it to sit a while, but it sold almost immediately. A cash buyer swooped in. He had been living out of a hotel while searching for a home in Danville and he wanted to close fast.

Too fast.

I was stunned. And panicked. I had no backup plan, no place to move, and two little pugs staring at me like, "So, where are we going now, Mom?"

Then my sister Jane stepped in. She offered her home in Rocklin to me and the dogs, sharing it with her husband, John, and their two boys, JR and Brenden, thirteen and nine, full of energy and mischief. I didn't hesitate for a second.

My nephews were thrilled. We had always gotten along well. I babysat them often and took them to Giants games whenever I could. There was an easy rhythm to our time together, a familiar comfort I knew I could count on.

I told Jane, "I'll be your nanny, your laundress, your cook, whatever you need." Truthfully, I was craving the feeling of family again, even if I was stepping into a temporary role.

I packed only the essentials, placed my furniture in storage, and prepared to move by the end of April. The plan was simple. Settle in, breathe, and decide what came next. Life wasn't stopping; it was simply turning a new page.

My last day at FIDM arrived with a heaviness I didn't expect. Admissions surprised me with a cake, and we gathered in the same conference room where we had held our Tuesday meetings for three decades. We laughed, cried, and shared stories, each memory a reminder of the life I had built within those walls.

Back in my office, students stopped in one by one to hug me and share how much I had meant to them. Their words wrapped around me gently, softening the ache building in my chest.

When it was time to go, I walked down the hallway to my director's office, handed over my key and badge, and we shared a tearful hug. Then I returned to my office one last time. I paused at the doorway, looking at the nameplate with my name on it, and felt thirty years wash over me in a single breath.

My mind drifted to some of the students who had gone on to do extraordinary things. Joie, for one, whose fashion label still graces the finest department stores, and though she's moved on to new ventures, her name remains a symbol of success. Then there was Wendy Benbrook, who once agonized over whether to pursue Visual Communications or Fashion Design. She chose Visual and went on to win two Emmys as costume designer for *Mad TV*. She even invited me backstage to a live taping of the show. Meeting the cast, along with Jeff Probst, fresh off his Emmy win for *Survivor*, was an unforgettable thrill. For years now she's been designing for the legendary rock band Kiss as well as other famous artists.

And then there was Louie. When he first appeared in my office fresh out of high school, I never imagined he would evolve into "Lucciano," a creative force of nature. He built a career as a producer and talent manager and became a close family friend long after graduation. His success was bold, but his loyalty was even brighter.

There were so many stories like theirs. Each student was a chapter in the book of my career. Every name, every face, every triumph became a thread in the tapestry of my life's work. Some arrived shy and uncertain; others came in bursting with ideas. All of them trusted me with their dreams and in return, they gave me purpose.

As I walked out the doors for the final time, I wasn't just leaving a job. I was carrying a lifetime of memories, lessons, and connections with me. They moved with me, step by step, a reminder that although this chapter had ended, the story we created together would always echo.

After leaving FIDM, I leaned into the comfort of the GF Club. Our wine nights and outings had slowed over the years as life pulled us in different directions, but the bond we created never faded. We were busy with new jobs and new commitments, but we made one promise. No matter what changed, we would stay connected. That vow became the quiet heartbeat of our friendship, a thread that held us close even when distance and time tried to pull us apart.

CHAPTER 26
SHORT TERM NANNY

I packed what I could, put furniture, too many clothes, and shoes into storage, and loaded my car with everything that would fit. The pugs and I spent our last night in Danville on an air mattress. That morning, after packing the last bits, I placed Rupert and Mona into their crates and started the drive to Rocklin. The road ahead was unclear, but the uncertainty didn't scare me.

Rupert, Mona, and I settled quickly at Jane and John's spacious two-story house. I was grateful my room was downstairs, which was perfect for me and the pugs. My nanny duties started immediately, and the daily rhythm took shape fast. Laundry. Lots of laundry. I'd been out of touch with the day-to-day of raising kids, but I didn't remember my girls going through that many clothes. Then again, my nephews, JR and Brenden, were in baseball gear nearly every day, which meant grass stains, red dirt, and socks galore. It felt endless, but I didn't mind.

It was comforting to be part of a busy household again. I became chauffeur, homework helper, and sports team supporter. I genuinely enjoyed it. It reminded me of my girls at that age—full of energy, attitude, and potential. I quizzed the boys before tests and was impressed by how sharp they were. Watching them grow felt like a quiet privilege. The boys loved having me there, and Rupert and Mona thrived on the attention.

Life had settled into a routine, and I wasn't in a rush to shake things up. Then, one afternoon, a recruiter reached out on LinkedIn. An aviation academy in Las Vegas was interested in my résumé, particularly my FIDM experience. They were looking for another admissions officer. After a few calls with the director, he invited me for an in-person visit. I figured, why not?

I reached out to Rick, a friend I'd reconnected with on Facebook. He and his girlfriend had moved to Las Vegas two years earlier and were loving it. Rick, a VIP at the Red Rock Casino Resort in Summerlin, offered a complimentary room. I accepted.

Rick picked me up from the airport and helped me check in. That evening, his girlfriend couldn't join us, so we dined alone. Rick raved about Summerlin, how peaceful it was compared to the Bay Area, and painted a picture of wine tastings, private dinners, and a relaxed pace.

The next day, I toured the aviation academy. The director greeted me warmly, described the position, and took me through the campus. At FIDM, I had been surrounded by fashion displays, dress forms, and young women buzzing with design dreams. Here, it was airplane hangars, cockpits, and young men training to be pilots and mechanics. It was a completely different world, yet fascinating. I didn't know if I'd take the job, but I was intrigued.

Back at Jane's, my head was spinning. The role mirrored my previous work in many ways, and while aviation wasn't fashion, it was compelling. The academy was interested in me, and we agreed to reconnect within the month.

In the meantime, I returned to nanny duties, enjoying the slower pace. No commute, no deadlines—just folding laundry, chauffeuring the boys, and watching them grow. I savored the mini-vacation from adult responsibilities.

Before the month ended, the academy invited me back to observe student interviews and get a feel for the culture. I agreed. I wanted to be sure. I booked another trip to Vegas for late August, and Rick arranged another stay at Red Rock. After shadowing the team, I could see myself in the role. It wasn't glamorous, but it felt meaningful. I felt useful and needed.

Rick kept pushing me toward Vegas. He drove me around Summerlin, a clean, upscale area that reminded me of Danville. He described wine clubs, tastings, and private dinners. Leaving California felt huge, but financially it made sense. Rent was far lower, and I could finally breathe.

He also encouraged me to look at housing. His friend Maryann, a local realtor, showed me a few homes. I told Rick I wasn't planning to move until next year, but he insisted it was just for perspective. I agreed.

We spent a day and a half touring houses. The prices were shocking. For the cost of a closet in the Bay Area, you could rent a mansion in Vegas.

Then I walked into *it.* A two-story beauty with three spacious bedrooms, room for family, space for all my Live for Pole merchandise, and a sparkling pool out back. It was perfect and available for $1,600 a month. In California, that wouldn't even get you a closet. I had planned to stay with Jane and John until the end of the year, but the house called to me. It felt meant to be. Moving alone was a leap. Aside from Rick, I didn't know a soul.

I took a breath and let the idea settle. That night, before leaving Vegas, the academy called. They offered me the job. I thanked the director and asked for a few days to think. The salary was lower than I was used to, but the cost of living made up for it.

Instead of jumping back into the workforce, I decided to pause and focus on something I'd been thinking about for a long time: my own business. I would pour myself into growing Live for Pole, give it the attention it deserved, and finally expand it the way I had always dreamed. I had big plans, including a sister site called Live for Chic, a fashion boutique to complement my brand. I wouldn't design the clothes, but I'd carefully curate and resell pieces I loved online. Six to eight months. That was my runway. It was finally time to bet on myself.

I didn't know exactly where I was headed yet, but I could feel it coming. The uncertainty was ending. Something new was calling, and I was ready to answer.

CHAPTER 27
LIGHTS, CAMERAS, ACTION

With my bags packed and business plans in motion, I traded California's traffic and sky-high prices for Las Vegas's oven blast, figuring if I was going to start fresh, I might as well do it somewhere my makeup could melt in record time. When the dogs and I arrived at the new house in Summerlin, Rick was already there, ready to greet us and help unload my car. My furniture wouldn't arrive until the next day, so that night I camped out on an air mattress.

The next day, the moving truck arrived. Within a couple of weeks, with everything in place, the house finally looked and felt like home.

Rick handled all the handyman work, hanging curtains, mounting pictures, and fixing little annoyances. I was grateful for the help, the company, and the way he eased the weight of such a big move. The bones of my new life were in place, and I was eager to start building it out with my next big project, launching my new online clothing store.

Rick couldn't wait to show me his favorite hangout, a bar called Rocks Lounge at the Red Rock Casino. He was a regular there, practically part of the furniture, and he knew all the bartenders and half the crowd by name. He introduced me as his "sis," which made me comfortable. No one needed to think we were a couple. By then, I knew he and his girlfriend had broken up, and she had moved back to California. I was surprised he hadn't mentioned it sooner, but I also wanted to make sure Rick didn't read anything romantic into our bond. He was like a brother to me and having that steady presence made the move and this new city feel less daunting.

I dove headfirst into building my Live for Chic website, and before long, orders started trickling in. Business was waking from its nap, and I was ready to roll. With a big pole convention coming up in a few months, I planned to bring inventory from both Live for Pole and Live for Chic. At past expos, vendors weren't just selling pole gear, they had regular fashion, too. So I figured, why not? I hunted down pieces pole dancers would drool over, including flashy dresses that said, "Look at me," silky kimonos to throw over a pole outfit when feeling mysterious, and stylish dresses, tops, jumpsuits, and other chic pieces for every occasion.

I also had cousins living in Vegas, including Carlos "Sonny" Padilla, the renowned referee from the famous Thrilla in Manila fight between Muhammad Ali and Joe Frazier. Meeting them in person for the first time was exciting but a little overwhelming. At the same time, I kept diving into my own projects. That spring, I attended a small pole convention and used it to test Live for Chic. To my surprise, it was a hit. Watching people light up over my pieces gave me a rush that shot straight through me and made me even more pumped for the big one later in the year, Pole Expo, run by the legendary Fawnia herself.

Meanwhile, my friend Donny, the PR whiz who helped me launch my Facebook pole page and pushed me to start my own clothing line, had also moved to Las Vegas. Not long after settling in, he hit me up with an unexpected opportunity. He was launching a live streaming show called *Vegas on Air* and wanted me to be the host. Interviewing people was kind of my thing. I could whip up questions in my sleep.

Donny's plan was simple. He would bring in clients looking to promote their businesses, and I would do live interviews. It was fun and eclectic. I ended up chatting with everyone from a pet food nutritionist and a party bus mogul to jewelry makers, chiropractors, Pilates instructors, and a Vegas chapel owner with themed chapels and a drive-through for quick "I do's."

Then came the highlight. I interviewed Fawnia Mondey, a pioneer of pole fitness, the world's first legitimate pole dance fitness instructor, and the powerhouse founder of Pole Expo. I had met her the year before as a vendor, and even then, she was personable. This time, I got to sit down and really talk with her. She was warm, friendly, and ridiculously approachable. We had a blast during our chat, and I even snagged footage of a class at her studio to give viewers a taste of the magic. That interview wasn't just fun; it reminded me how incredible the pole world had become to me.

Just when I was settling into my groove, I got a call from the aviation academy. The director hadn't forgotten about me and was looking for an assistant director for admissions. I was flattered, but I needed more time to build my empire and enjoy life without the soul-crushing daily commute. We made a deal. I would start at the end of October. Perfect timing. By then, I would be ready to trade sweatpants for serious work shoes.

Looking back, those early months in Vegas were a whirlwind but necessary in ways I didn't yet understand. They laid the foundation I needed at a moment when my life was changing in more ways than I could see. I was still finding my footing in the city and in myself. I didn't know what the future held, but for the first time in a long while, I felt open to it.

What I didn't see then was the weight tucked quietly beneath the whirlwind, patient and unspoken, waiting for its moment.

CHAPTER 28
EMBRACING SUCCESS WITH A HEAVY HEART

Even so, I kept moving forward. And at the time, that was enough to keep going. The whirlwind of early Vegas had given me the confidence to dive into something I loved. By September, that energy carried me straight to Pole Expo. I was beyond excited to showcase my expanded merchandise at my booth. Once again, I secured a prime spot right by the stage, where foot traffic never stopped. The event buzzed with dancers performing all day, workshops in full swing, and shoppers eager to browse.

Sales? A total hit. The crowd devoured Live for Chic just as enthusiastically as Live for Pole.

What really made my heart swell, though, was how the pole community was starting to recognize me, not just as a vendor, but as a person. Thanks to my Facebook pole page, dancers from all over the world came up to introduce themselves. It was a warm, affirming feeling. I couldn't help but flash back to my younger years, when I had felt invisible or worse, the target of sneers and snickers. This was my "Take a look at me now" moment, and I soaked it all in with a huge, grateful smile.

The success gave me a boost of confidence and a sense of ease as I prepared to start my new adventure at the aviation academy at the end of October. Little did I know that I would never quite make it to that first day.

The event was a hit, and my heart was full—but outside the lights and applause, life reminded me it was never that simple. A shadow of guilt and sadness crept in. Both Jun and Jane had been recently diagnosed—Jun with prostate cancer and Jane with breast cancer, which she learned about while I was still living with them and preparing for my move to Vegas. I felt a heavy weight of guilt knowing I was leaving them behind during such a difficult time. Even amid my own victories, it was impossible to ignore how illness and loss had touched those I loved.

Then there was Maribel, my niece from my previous marriage to Manny. His family was still very much a part of my life. She was battling kidney disease fiercely. Her latest transplant was failing, and she was frequently in and out of the hospital. When she and her family—her husband and two teenage boys—came to Vegas to visit her father, who was in rehab following a stroke, I invited them to stay at my home.

Seeing her so fragile broke my heart. She couldn't climb the stairs; she had to be carried by her husband. That image stayed with me long after they left. The overwhelming sadness wasn't just for Maribel; it was for all those struggling around me.

My heart told me I couldn't do nothing. I had been blessed with good health, a fit body, and a stable home. It only felt right to share that blessing. So I made the decision to donate a kidney to Maribel.

I gave it a lot of thought and even prayed about it. Deep down, I knew this was something I had to do. I told Maribel right away, and though she was incredibly grateful, she warned me the approval process would be tough. But I was determined. I made every appointment and went through all the tests, eager to find out if we were compatible. I wanted nothing more than to give her, a young mother battling so much, a chance at a pain-free life.

When the results came back and I was told I wasn't a good candidate because of my high blood pressure, my heart sank. It was a crushing moment.

I still needed to feel like I was making a difference, like I was doing something meaningful amid the weight pressing on my heart. Junior, Maribel's father and my former brother-in-law, was in a rehab facility in Vegas after his stroke, isolated from the rest of his family who were all back in California. I began visiting him almost every other day, needing that connection as much as he did.

On days when I couldn't be there myself, I would pick up his girlfriend in the morning, take her to spend the day with him, and then bring her home again in the evening. I cleaned his apartment. I sat with him during long stretches of silence, consulted with the nurses, and helped navigate the confusing world of insurance and medical paperwork.

In those moments, I felt a fragile thread of purpose weaving through the heaviness I carried. Helping him gave me a way to channel the helplessness and sadness that threatened to consume me. Being there for Junior wasn't just about caring for him; it was about healing parts of myself I hadn't known were broken.

The weight in my chest lifted just a little, reminding me that even in the hardest times, kindness and presence can be a lifeline.

Even amid the giving and caring, the quiet ache inside me lingered, a shadow tucked beneath the surface, waiting for its moment. For now, I could push it aside, focus on the people and projects that mattered, and keep moving forward. But deep down, I knew it was still there, patiently watching, a reminder that strength and struggle often walk hand in hand.

CHAPTER 29
MOM

Back in California, life continued to unravel in ways I could not control. My siblings were already deep in their own battles, and Mom's health was steadily declining. She was in and out of the hospital, and we eventually moved her from assisted living to a nursing home with full-time care. The staff, many of them Filipino nurses, treated her with warmth and familiarity, and she seemed comfortable there. Still, at ninety-three, time was no longer on her side.

I flew back whenever I could. I visited Mom and stayed with Jane during her surgery. I felt guilty for not being there through her chemo, but I made the trips as often as possible. In early May, Mom took a sharp turn for the worse, and I went back again, determined to spend whatever time we had left together. Eventually, it became clear that it was her time. We made the painful choice to place her in hospice care at the same home where she had been living.

During that final visit, I saw all three of them together. Jun was weakened from his treatments. Jane hid her bare head beneath a soft scarf. Mom drifted in and out of awareness. None of us could bring ourselves to tell her that two of her children were battling cancer. Some truths only add weight to a heart that is already heavy.

Eventually, it was time for me to return to Vegas. Business matters needed my attention, and I was preparing to start a new job, one I was genuinely excited about. I threw myself into organizing everything so my businesses would keep moving forward, never imagining that I would never get to walk through the doors of the aviation academy.

Before I left California, I spent one last afternoon with Mom. She was having a good day. Her eyes lit up when she recognized me, and we reminisced about old times. Her strength and spark were deceptive. I knew these bursts of energy often came just before exhaustion set in.

As I rose to leave, I held her hand, bent down, and kissed her cheek. "I have to go back home," I whispered.

She looked at me and asked softly, "When are you coming back?"

"Soon, Mom. Very soon," I said, forcing a smile as tears slipped down my face, knowing it would be the very last time I would see her alive.

Back in Vegas, the silence of my home pressed in on me. I curled up with my dogs, burying my face in their fur, searching for comfort in their steady warmth. But no matter how tightly I held them, the heaviness in my heart refused to lift.

The following Sunday, my siblings, my daughters, Aunt Mila, Mom's sister, and I were all group texting, but I had to turn my phone off during church service. When it ended and I walked to my car, I turned my phone back on. It was buzzing nonstop with missed messages. One stood out, bold and unmistakable, from Aunt Mila: "She's gone."

My heart sank. I had been bracing myself for this moment, but nothing could have prepared me for how deeply it hit. I slid into the driver's seat and sat there for what felt like forever, tears streaming down my face as the weight of loss settled over me.

I flew back for Mom's celebration of life. It was a heartfelt and beautiful gathering. Funerals have a bittersweet way of reuniting friends and family you have not seen in years, sometimes decades. Seeing them again warmed my heart, yet it also stirred a quiet guilt for feeling happiness in the middle of grief.

The day after the service, I returned to Vegas. I took one day to rest, then boarded a plane to Chicago. Kristin, Ashley, and I had planned a trip months earlier. It was our first time visiting the Windy City, and we were going to see a Giants versus Cubs game. I flew in separately to meet the girls, who were coming from California.

We explored the city and indulged in its famous food scene. The Giants lost, but it hardly mattered. The trip gave us exactly what we needed, a brief escape that reminded us joy is still possible, even in the darkest seasons.

Growing up, I often felt unloved and unwanted. Over time, though, I began to understand that my mom expressed love in her own way. Somewhere near the end, my understanding deepened in a way I never expected. I went from feeling invisible to sensing that I might have been the one she loved the most. It sounds unbelievable, yet it is exactly how it felt. As if all her quiet, tough love had been saved for me.

In those final moments, I felt an overwhelming surge of love from her, almost like a silent plea. Please forgive me for the times I made you feel invisible, neglected, and unloved.

By then, years of distance and misunderstanding had softened into something unspoken but deeply understood. Love, imperfect and late, had finally found its way to me. It arrived quietly, without grand gestures, like a long-lost letter finally reaching its destination. In its own tough and tender way, it was both a benediction and a farewell.

Her passing closed a chapter, yet her presence still lingers. It reminds me that love is not always loud or easy to recognize, but it shapes us nonetheless, revealing itself long after the storm has passed.

CHAPTER 30
BETWEEN HEARTBEATS

Loss has a way of making time feel fragile, like everything meaningful happens in the space between one breath and the next. After Mom passed, I threw myself into activity, believing staying occupied would help me survive the sadness that threatened to pull me under. Even as life seemed full and exciting, a quiet shadow of grief lingered, a reminder that loss doesn't leave us entirely. By early October 2017, things appeared to be falling into place.

Both of my online clothing stores, Live for Pole and Live for Chic, were humming along. Sales were not sky-high, but they were steady enough to provide a little extra cash, a cushion I wanted before starting my new role at the aviation academy at the end of the month. Hosting Vegas on Air kept me connected and entertained, a side hustle that brought a spark of excitement to my days, even as the lingering sadness occasionally returned in moments I least expected.

One afternoon, while enjoying the familiar buzz of the Red Rock Casino buffet, my footing betrayed me. I slipped on a slick patch of salad dressing and fell hard, jolting my back in a way that made even breathing painful. Sneezing, coughing, every tiny movement sent sharp jolts through my spine. This was not pain I could ignore.

Insurance was a problem. I had a minimal health plan, affordable but limited. It covered the basics, and since I had been in good health for years, I had not expected medical emergencies. Aside from high blood pressure, which my medication kept in check, I had no reason to be concerned. With my new job and its better benefits just around the corner, I figured I could hold on a little longer.

Determined to get the care I needed, I contacted an attorney to see if I could recoup treatment costs. They were encouraging, telling me I had a strong case, and connected me with a chiropractor willing to take me on contingency. No upfront cost unless we won. It was a lifeline I needed.

I started chiropractic treatments three times a week, hoping for relief. By the second week, the pain exploded from a manageable seven to a brutal twenty-five on a scale of one to ten. Every breath and step was torture. Ibuprofen did nothing. I arrived at my appointment in tears, exhausted and desperate.

The chiropractor did what he could, but he could not prescribe medication. He wrote a referral to the medical office next door, explaining they could handle prescriptions. I was counting on finally getting some real relief.

When the doctor came in, she did not rush to ease my suffering. Instead, she checked my vitals and listened to my heart. Then she asked, "Do you know you have a heart murmur?"

I had no idea, and that was not why I was there. I thought my regular doctor in Vegas would have mentioned it if I had one. I explained that I had a doctor there for my blood pressure medication, but what I needed was help with my back. She ordered an EKG right away.

When she returned with the EKG results, she told me I needed to see my primary care doctor immediately. I barely registered the urgency. All I wanted was a prescription to take the edge off this unbearable pain. I asked if she could write one in the meantime. She shook her head.

"No. You have to call your doctor right away. Tell them about the murmur and this visit. They will see you immediately."

Disappointed, I called my primary doctor, who told me to come in right away. On the drive over, I held onto the hope that she might help with the pain while sorting out the murmur. But the pain was crushing.

At the office, I was taken straight to an exam room. Usually there was a half-hour wait, even with an appointment. I gave my doctor a full rundown of everything since my last visit six months earlier and begged for relief. The lower back pain felt a thousand times worse than labor.

But like the other doctor, her first move was to listen to my heart. I saw the concern in her eyes. This murmur was new to her, too. Without ordering another EKG, she told me I needed to go to the ER immediately at the hospital across the street. I could not believe it. Again, my pleas for pain relief were being sidelined.

Tears streamed down my face. Even though she seemed genuinely worried about my heart, I could not spare a thought for it. My lower back was screaming for help.

I told her I needed to get home first to feed my dogs, then I would go to the hospital. She cut me off firmly. This could not wait. She instructed me to tell the ER staff I was having chest pains and difficulty breathing.

I blinked, confused. "But that is not true. My chest does not hurt, and I can breathe fine. It is my back that hurts."

She looked me straight in the eyes. "Janette, please say exactly what I told you. That way, they will see you immediately, and they can give you something for your pain right away."

That was all I needed to hear. I climbed into my car, but before heading across the street, I called Rick. I asked if he could go to my house and feed my dogs. He told me not to worry and hoped it was nothing serious. Thank goodness I could count on him.

At the ER check-in window, I repeated exactly what my doctor told me: "I am having chest pains and difficulty breathing. I just came from my doctor across the street. She heard a heart murmur I did not have before."

Just like that, I was taken straight to the back. They listened to my heart, ran an EKG, and drew blood. I told them about my back injury and the unbearable pain. They injected something into my vein that instantly stopped the back pain. Relief washed over me. I felt elated. My heart faded from my thoughts. For the first time in days, I was relaxed.

After a while, a nurse came in with news. It seemed I had suffered a series of mini heart attacks, or so they suspected. It was late evening, and they admitted me for monitoring. A cardiologist would see me first thing in the morning.

I sent a message in "Cougar Chat," a group which included my daughters, sisters, and my niece. We had kept that group chat for years, a lifeline of constant banter, updates, and love. Kristin, my daughter, had named it Cougar Chat, a playful nod to us "older siblings" that always made us laugh.

When I told them what the doctor said, the chat instantly turned serious. My daughters were alarmed, convinced I had gone through a series of mini heart attacks. They wanted to fly out immediately and be in Vegas that night. I reassured them the worst had passed. "I am fine," I insisted. "Just come tomorrow after work, and you won't have to take too much time off." Still, I could feel their worry.

After that, I called Rick again and asked him to feed the dogs in the morning and let them out to relieve themselves. He did not hesitate. I didn't have many friends in Vegas yet, no one to really lean on. Knowing Rick was there was a blessing.

That night, I barely drifted off before the agony ripped me awake. The same stabbing, twisting lower back pain returned with a vengeance.

I hit the call button so hard I thought I might break it. The nurse walked in calmly, and I begged for the same shot that had erased the pain earlier.

His face did not change. "Cardiologist's orders. No more meds until he sees you in the morning."

The words detonated inside me. I screamed. My voice came out jagged and feral, words flying that I barely recognized. The pain clamped around my lower back like a vice, twisting tighter with every breath.

He backed away and said he would call the doctor. I was left writhing, shaking, my heart pounding against my ribs.

When he returned, he could not meet my eyes. "The doctor approved Tylenol."

"Tylenol?" The word exploded from me. "Are you kidding me?"

I took it because I had no choice. Then I lay there in the dark, praying those useless pills would do something before the pain swallowed me whole.

Miraculously, I must have slipped into a restless sleep, because when I finally opened my eyes, it was to the soft click of the door and a new nurse quietly entering my room. Relief surfaced for a moment. Maybe this time would be different. But as soon as the familiar ache in my lower back flared awake, I knew the battle was far from over.

I pleaded with her, desperation creeping into my voice, begging for something stronger than the Tylenol I had been given before. Surely she wouldn't deny me the relief I so desperately needed. But she returned apologetically with more Tylenol, the same gentle pills that barely touched the edge of my pain.

I felt rage bubbling up again, ready to break through. My body screamed with every breath, and it felt cruel to be handed the gentlest medicine while trapped in the worst pain of my life. I was about to unleash another tirade when she paused and lowered her voice. The cardiologist would be here soon. He was already making rounds.

That small hint of hope kept me from falling apart completely. Maybe he would see what I was going through and finally help me.

When the cardiologist entered, the entire room felt different. His presence was calm and steady, a contrast to the storm raging inside my body. He listened patiently as I explained the agony in my back and the frustration of being caught between fear and pain, trapped between caution and desperation.

He explained that he was not convinced I had suffered any heart attacks at all. The news surprised me, and for a moment, it lifted something heavy inside me. Not just for my heart, but for the possibility that he might finally address the real reason I was falling apart.

I asked for the one thing I craved, the magical shot that had erased the pain before. His answer was gentle but firm. It was too soon for stronger medications, and I would need to continue with Tylenol until they could confirm it was safe. An echo test had already been ordered and an ultrasound of my heart scheduled for 11:00 a.m.

It was only 7:30 in the morning.

I lay there in disbelief, wondering how I would survive the next few hours. Every minute felt like an eternity. I tried to breathe through the stabbing pulses of pain, gripping the sides of the bed just to stay grounded, waiting for time to pass.

Shortly after the doctor left, my phone buzzed. It was Fawnia. Yes, that Fawnia. Founder of Pole Expo and the world's first legitimate pole fitness instructor, a woman whose name carried weight wherever pole dancers gathered. I stared at the screen to make sure I wasn't imagining it.

Apparently, my daughters and siblings had posted about what was happening to me on Facebook, and word had spread quickly. Fawnia wanted to visit me. Today. In the middle of her packed schedule, she was offering to sit with me in a hospital room. I felt a rush of shock and gratitude. I told her I had a test at eleven, and she could come anytime around then. Just imagining her walking in sent a small wave of comfort through the pain.

Before that surprise could settle, my phone rang again. It was Bel. Mama Bel. The owner of Twirly Girls, my first pole instructor, the one who taught me my earliest spins and gave me my first glimpses of strength. Her voice wrapped around me like a hug. She told me she had a close friend in Vegas, someone I had never met, who wanted to come sit with me. The thought stopped me in my tracks. I didn't know her, but she was willing to spend her day in a hospital just so I would not be alone.

I felt a sharp stab of pain bolt through my lower back. The Tylenol had not dulled it at all. Yet here were people reaching across cities and schedules without hesitation. Strangers stepping into my world simply to offer comfort.

It humbled me. It softened something in me that had been hardening under the constant weight of fear, pain, and the lingering shadows of grief.

I endured the echo test, gritting my teeth every time the technician repositioned me. The gel was cold, and every movement sent a fresh burst of pain tearing through my back. I tried to focus on her calm instructions, on the rhythmic swish of my heartbeat echoing through the machine, but the pain kept pulling me under.

Finally, she turned off the monitor and began wheeling her cart toward the door.

That was when I saw her.

She lingered just outside the doorway, a quiet force of grace and strength, as if the hospital itself had paused for her.

Fawnia.

She stepped in, her presence filling the room like sunlight breaking through heavy clouds. She wore black jeans and the Live for Pole hoodie I had once given her. Seeing her in it felt like the universe handing me a reminder: You are not alone. For the first time that morning, my body unclenched just a little.

Moments later, the door swung open again, and in came Mich, Bel's friend I'd never met. She was pure light, her smile chasing away whatever shadows Fawnia hadn't already cleared. In her hands was a small care package: a toothbrush, toothpaste, ChapStick, soft Kleenex, and a stack of glossy tabloid magazines. The simple, thoughtful things you don't realize you need until someone cares enough to bring them.

I introduced Mich to Fawnia, and just like that, the sterile, mechanical hum of the hospital room softened into something warmer, safer. It felt almost like I'd been rescued.

We chatted, sharing stories and laughter that felt like balm on my weary soul. At one point, I glanced at the wall clock and noticed the time was wrong. Fawnia, ever the problem-solver, carefully took the giant clock down and tried to adjust it. After a while, it was clear the battery was dead. Somehow, that simple malfunction cracked us up, and the three of us dissolved into laughter, filling the sterile room with warmth and life.

By then, it was well past 2:00 p.m. They had stayed with me for nearly two hours, turning a painful, exhausting day into something bearable. When it was finally time to say goodbye, they each gave me a heartfelt hug. I thanked them from the bottom of my heart for coming when I needed it most.

The moment the door closed, reality rushed back. During their visit, the back pain had faded into the background, almost as if it respected their company. But now, alone again, the relentless ache crept back, settling deep into my muscles and bones. Still, those two hours had given me a precious reprieve—a reminder that even in the darkest moments, kindness and laughter can find their way in.

After the ladies left, Rick stopped by. He did not stay long, but I filled him in on everything. We were still waiting on the echo results before anyone would address the back pain. I reminded him he would need to swing by my house again later to feed the dogs and let them out. It struck me how, even while hospitalized, my attention remained fixed on the stabbing pain in my lower back. The heart murmur, the supposedly serious heart issue, still had not fully registered.

Not long after Rick left, the room settled into an uneasy quiet. The steady beeping of the monitor seemed louder now, as if it were marking time for something I could not yet see coming. My chest felt tight, each breath slightly shallower than the last. My back still ached, but my thoughts kept circling one question. Why was everyone moving with such unspoken urgency around me?

Footsteps approached. A nurse appeared in the doorway holding a cordless phone. Her expression was calm, but her eyes were sharp.

"Your cardiologist is on the line. He needs to speak with you right away."

I sat up straighter, my pulse spiking. A faint metallic taste spread across my tongue as I took the phone.

"Hello?"

His voice was calm, almost too calm. "I got the results from your echocardiogram, Janette. My suspicions were confirmed. You have not had any heart attacks."

Hope passed through me. Maybe now they could give me real pain medication and send me home. But before I could exhale, his tone changed.

"It is much worse."

My chest tightened.

"One of your heart valves, your mitral valve, has completely collapsed. Your lungs are filling with fluid. Your kidneys are starting to shut down. The pain in your lower back is not from your fall. It is your kidneys failing."

I blinked hard, trying to make the words line up. My palms grew damp. My legs felt hollow beneath the blanket.

"You need emergency open heart surgery to replace your valve," he continued. "Before we can operate, you will need an angiogram. The dye could further damage your kidneys, but it is necessary. We cannot operate without knowing the exact condition of your coronary arteries."

My daughters were flying in from California that evening. Kristin and Ashley were arriving at different times. I asked if we could wait until they got there.

His response was immediate and firm.

"Janette, listen carefully. You will not survive through the night without this surgery. I have already contacted the surgeon. He is on his way. I am heading back to the hospital now."

The phone slipped from my hand. The nurse picked it up and stepped out, still speaking to him. When she returned, she carried a stack of forms, her expression grave. The surgery was imperative. My eyes skimmed the pages, but one word leapt out again and again.

Risk.

Shaking, I called my brother-in-law John, a firefighter and former paramedic, hoping he could make sense of the nightmare unfolding. I was nearly incoherent as I repeated the doctor's words. He stayed calm and steady and told me I had to do it.

I signed the forms.

Then I called Rick and my Vegas on Air partner, Donny, to tell them what was happening. Without hesitation, Rick offered to pick up Ashley from the airport. Donny said he would get Kristin since they were arriving at different times.

Before the gurney arrived, I made my way to the nurses' station and asked for paper and an envelope. Back in my room, I wrote a letter to Kristin and Ashley, just in case I did not wake up. I included instructions about my bank accounts and the cash I had hidden at home. My hands trembled so badly I had to stop twice. When I finished, I tucked the letter into my belongings and prayed they would never have to find it.

A couple of hours later, the gurney came. First the angiogram, then the valve replacement. The upside, if there was one, was the injection they gave me that erased every trace of pain. I felt giddy, loose, almost lighthearted.

As the young men wheeled me toward the operating room, I looked up at them and, for reasons I still cannot explain, blurted out, "I do not usually look like this. In fact, I am a pole dancer."

I cannot believe I said that. I cannot believe I remember it. But I do remember their smiles.

That was the last thing I saw before everything went black.

CHAPTER 31
SHADOWS AND BEEPS

As I drifted in and out of consciousness, the sterile hospital room warped into a nightmare that felt painfully real. The beeping machines were no longer just machines; they were ticking bombs, each pulse hammering frantic warnings through my skull. The nurses, once calm and kind, twisted into shadowy figures lurking just beyond my vision, holding me captive. Every breath felt like a countdown to disaster, every beep a signal that time was running out. I was trapped, helpless, imprisoned by my own terrified mind.

Then I heard a voice, cold and distant: "She's waking up." My eyes flew open, but panic swallowed me whole. I tried to scream, but only a broken, hoarse rasp emerged, like the sounds I had made during past kidnappings. My arms flailed uncontrollably, thrashing, trying to break free. This was not a hospital room. It was a cage. Third time's the nightmare. The walls closed in. My chest constricted like a vise, each breath a fragile thread slipping through my grasp. The air grew thin and heavy, and my thoughts scattered like leaves in a storm, wild and uncontrollable.

I looked up at the giant wall clock. Nine o'clock. I asked for my daughters and was told they were not there yet. Each time I asked, the answer was the same. I gasped and begged, voice cracking, "Where are they?" Only silence came back. Abandonment crashed over me like a wave of ice water, numbing everything. My eyes found the clock again, that big, unforgiving clock. Nine o'clock. Always nine o'clock. Every blink, every breath, it stared back, frozen and merciless. Time had stopped, trapping me in a nightmare I could not escape.

Sleep dragged me under again, but every time I surfaced, the panic intensified. The machines were bombs ticking louder and louder, ready to destroy me. The nurses became threats standing in the shadows, watching, waiting. I screamed for water. My throat burned like fire. A cold, wet sponge brushed my lips, then was yanked away before I could taste any relief. Nine o'clock. No movement. No mercy.

My heart hammered against my ribs. I whispered, trembling, "They're not who they seem. You have to be careful. The machines are bombs. They could blow us up any second. We need to get out. Now." My daughters' worried eyes searched mine, but terror blurred their faces. I reached for them, trying to pull them close, but the room stretched and twisted, pushing everything further away. Reality and nightmare tangled together, and I was trapped inside both.

Time slipped through my fingers like sand. The clock remained frozen at nine o'clock, mocking me as the beeping grew louder and more insistent. I was caught in a world that made no sense, where every shadow hid danger and every sound threatened destruction. All I could do was beg them to run, to escape the terror I could not fight.

I do not know how long I stayed like that. Hours, days, an eternity. Time had no meaning. Every time I forced my eyes open, the clock stared back at me. Nine o'clock. Always nine o'clock. The steady beep pulsed in my ears like a countdown, but the hands never moved. I was trapped in a loop where nothing changed, yet everything slipped away.

The panic clawed at me with the same choking terror I had known during the kidnappings. Only now there were no ropes, no speeding car, no cold hands holding me down. I was tied to the bed by my own failing body, surrounded by strangers who moved like shadows, their faces cold and foreign.

Apparently, I was in and out of consciousness for the first few days after surgery. Then, like a faint light breaking through a storm, I saw my sister Jane. Her head was wrapped tightly in a scarf that concealed the softness of her shaved scalp, a silent reminder of the battles she fought far from mine. She sat quietly beside me, a steady presence in a sea of confusion. I do not remember us speaking, but I felt her there, an anchor keeping me connected to the world.

The next few days were a blur of shadows and whispers. I was in the ICU, where I remained for the first week. I drifted in and out of consciousness, my mind trapped behind fogged glass. Conversations floated around me, bits of worry and love I could not grasp. It was like being held captive by my own body, the walls closing in tighter each day.

After the weekend, Jane and Kristin flew home. Their goodbyes were soft, weighed down by unspoken fears. I hated watching them leave, knowing their hearts were breaking as much as mine. Ashley stayed, a quiet guardian. Caring for my dogs at home, working remotely, and still finding time to be by my side every day. Her presence was a lifeline, proof that beyond the sterile hospital walls, life and love still waited.

After a few days, I began staying awake longer. That is when the truth of what I had endured—and what lay ahead—settled in. Recovery would not be quick. It would not be "typical." Four of my chordae tendineae, the delicate strings holding the mitral valve in place, had snapped when my valve collapsed, making the road back even steeper. My kidneys had not escaped damage either, forcing me into dialysis.

Even heavily medicated, I clung to small threads of connection. Ashley would read Facebook messages to me, and I could check texts when I had the energy. Love poured in from every direction. Flowers were not allowed in the ICU, but balloons were, and my room became a riot of color. One evening, maybe it was the medication, maybe it was something else, I fixated on a yellow smiley-face balloon hovering in front of me. In my mind, it transformed into Mom. Her presence folded into the room. I spoke softly to it, sharing thoughts as if she were really there. It was warm, comforting, a fragile haven of solace amid the storm.

Food offered no comfort. Water tasted like rust, soup like pennies, juice like something poured from an old pipe. But the blueberry smoothies Ashley smuggled from home were different. Cold, creamy, bursting with the sweet-tart pop of fresh blueberries, they slid down my throat like silk, waking taste buds that had forgotten what joy tasted like. Every sip was a tiny rebellion against the metallic sludge the hospital offered, a frozen blue lifeline in the middle of all that gray.

CHAPTER 32
SHAMPOO

By my second week, the filth in my hair was driving me mad. I begged a nurse to help me wash it.

She smiled and said, "Let's do it," and returned with shampoo. With another nurse's help, she wheeled me into the bathroom and lifted me just high enough over the sink to let warm water cascade through my tangled hair. It felt like heaven, steam curling around my face, the scent of shampoo cutting through the antiseptic air.

Then Ashley appeared in the doorway, her smile fading as her eyes dropped to the floor.

"Is that your blood?" she asked.

We froze. Our gaze followed hers, and there it was, a huge pool of blood spreading across the tile. There was more than I had ever seen in my life, dark and glossy under the harsh bathroom light. A trail led straight to my groin, where a tube hung loosely. My mind raced. I suddenly remembered earlier, straining on the toilet. The pressure had forced the tube out.

One of the nurses shouted to the student nurse, who raced out and returned almost immediately with a massive orderly. My vision blurred, my legs wobbled, and a wave of dizziness slammed into me. I was probably on the edge of fainting from the blood loss. My chest hammered in my ribcage, my throat was parched, and the metallic tang of blood made my stomach churn. The crimson tide pooling across the floor was horrifying, making my heart pound harder, my fear spike higher.

The nurse pressed her hand firmly over the gaping hole in my groin, every pulse reverberating through me. I felt utterly fragile, my body betraying me, trembling in terror. The orderly lifted me with a grunt, every muscle quivering, my mind teetering on the edge of blacking out. How could this even be happening? My arms felt like lead. My world tilted with every movement. I was completely at the mercy of these strangers, yet a thread of trust, maybe the only thing keeping me grounded, remained.

They laid me on the bed, cold sheets brushing against my fevered skin, and the nurse worked swiftly, cleaning and bandaging with deliberate care. The orderly who had carried me was covered in my blood, his scrubs dark and smeared as if he had just stepped out of a battlefield. My body shook, I felt faint, but my mind, despite the fear, clung to one absurd detail: my hair. Somehow, through all that chaos, it was still clean. That small, ordinary victory felt impossibly enormous.

CHAPTER 33
FROM BALLOONS TO TEARS

I was encouraged to stroll the hallways with a walker, each step helping my blood circulate and reminding me that my body was still capable of movement, even if it felt monumental.

One afternoon, after I'd started shuffling around in baby steps, a nurse appeared in my doorway. "Hi," she said. "I just wanted to check in and see how you're doing. I was one of the nurses who took care of you in the ICU."

"I think I'm doing okay," I told her, "But honestly, I don't really know."

She tilted her head, studying me. "You don't remember me, do you?"

"No… should I?"

She grinned, a teasing glint in her eye. "You told me that, on a scale of one to ten in fashion, I was a three."

I stared at her, horrified. That was so unlike me. I would never say something like that on purpose. She chuckled and reassured me, "It's okay, really. I know it wasn't you talking. The medication can do strange things."

"Oh no… I'm so sorry," I said, my face flushing. "It must have been the medication talking. I promise, I think you're at least an eight."

A couple of days later, as I was doing another slow lap around the floor, I spotted her again at the nurses' station. This time, I stopped and gave her an exaggerated once-over.

"Hmm," I said, pretending to evaluate her outfit like a red-carpet critic. "I've decided I was wrong before. Today you're at least a nine. Possibly a nine and a half with that colorful hoodie."

She burst out laughing, and a couple of other nurses turned to see what was so funny. "Good to know my style is improving," she said, playing along.

It was a small, silly moment, but after everything—the fear, the pain, the days lost in a medicated fog—it felt good to share a laugh.

My dialysis sessions were always late at night, so I was usually fast asleep while hooked up to the machines, blissfully unaware of the world around me. After many sessions, the readings showed improvement. The doctor said that if my kidney function stayed stable, I could be discharged in the next few days. The thought of leaving the hospital felt almost surreal. It was Halloween, and Ashley brought in a huge box of donuts for the nurses' station. They were thrilled, and their laughter filled the floor, adding a touch of warmth to the otherwise sterile environment.

I was feeling surprisingly good and hopeful that this might finally be the day I could go home. By now, I was walking two slow laps around the floor with my walker, each step a small victory. Most of the other patients were older than me, and some even questioned why I was there, remarking that I looked so young. They were more than happy to chat, and I found their stories amusing. Talking with them helped pass the time, and I laughed quietly at their quirks and observations. The little moments of humanity in a place that could feel so clinical and impersonal meant more than I'd realized.

The only other entertainment came from the World Series. Los Angeles Dodgers versus Houston Astros. As an avid San Francisco Giants fan, I couldn't help but root for the Astros.

The next day, I got the best news ever: I was being discharged that evening. They still needed to keep an eye on my vitals during the day, but if everything stayed steady, I'd be out after dinner. I was already picturing the bliss of my own bed when someone came in to talk with me and Ashley. That's when I learned I wouldn't be going home yet. Instead, I was being sent to a rehab facility. They were just waiting for a bed to open up. Honestly,

I didn't think much of it. I figured it would be like a hotel with physical therapy, maybe even a spa robe. But it wasn't.

The call came. My bed was ready. All that was left was to wait for medical transportation since Ashley wasn't allowed to drive me herself. We killed time watching Game 7 of the Dodgers–Astros World Series. When the transport team arrived, two easygoing guys joined us. They were Dodgers haters too, so there was plenty of friendly trash talk while we waited.

After three weeks at this hospital, my room looked like a birthday party for a small parade float. I had over two dozen balloons—big ones, small ones, metallic ones that caught the light, and shimmery ribbons that swayed whenever the air conditioner kicked on. They had been with me through long nights, searing pain, and the relentless beeping of machines. A quiet, floating audience to my recovery. In a strange, inexplicable way, they became my companions, my silent witnesses, tiny guardians who had seen me through some of the scariest moments of my life.

Just like Wilson in Castaway, they had been my lifeline when everything else felt uncertain, an anchor of comfort and hope. Sometimes I even caught myself whispering little updates to them, imagining that they nodded along, cheering me on in their own silent way.

Saying goodbye to them as I left the hospital felt heavier than I expected. My chest tightened with a pang of sadness. These balloons had been more than decoration. They had been my confidants, my invisible cheer squad through nights filled with pain and fear. I made sure Ashley saved the yellow smiley-face one—the balloon I believed was Mom. She grabbed a few others to take home so they would be waiting for me when I finally returned. Leaving the rest behind to be donated to other patients was the right thing to do, but it felt like leaving a piece of my journey behind. Still, I took comfort imagining them drifting into someone else's day, bringing a spark of joy just as they had buoyed me.

The two attendants wheeled me out to the ambulance, and I cranked up my phone so we could listen to Game 7. They were both Dodgers haters and cracked jokes the whole way, which made the ride a little easier. Ashley followed behind in the car.

When we arrived at the rehab facility, it was a whole different ballgame, and not in a good way. This place was nothing like Summerlin Hospital, and I would have much preferred to stay there. We rolled through the front doors past a nurses' station, but no one looked up. No hello. No good evening. Not even a glance. The hallways were lined with patients—some asleep, some staring blankly, others murmuring to themselves. My stomach sank. I hated it before I'd even taken a step inside.

The attendants seemed to know where they were going and brought me straight into a room. It was already occupied by an older woman near the door. My bed was tucked in the far corner. She took one look at me, shook her head, and said, "Don't you put anything in that cabinet there," pointing to the dresser beside my bed. I just nodded as they lifted me onto my bed.

There was a TV in my corner, so Ashley, the attendants, and I watched the final plays of the game. We cheered when the Astros defeated the Dodgers. Then the attendants wished me luck and left, and the loneliness hit like a wave.

Ashley and I looked around. The room was drab and worn, with only a curtain separating me from a roommate who clearly resented my being there. I would have given anything for my private room back at Summerlin, where everything was clean and sterile. Here, the air felt heavy, and the place looked like it was overdue for a deep cleaning.

I told Ashley I couldn't stay. She went to find someone, anyone, since no one had greeted us when we came in and no one had checked on me since. She returned saying she'd tried to get me moved to a private room, but none were available.

Someone followed Ashley in to take my vitals and chat briefly. Then another person arrived with more questions. The vibe here was completely different—less care, less warmth. It was getting late.

Ashley asked if she could just take me home, but they said without a proper discharge, I wouldn't get my medication, something I desperately needed. They told us someone would assess me the next day and decide when I could go home.

By then, it was almost 11:00 p.m. Ashley had to leave. I tried to be brave, but as soon as she walked out, I broke. I cried so hard I could barely breathe. Just hours earlier, I had been ecstatic, thinking I was going home. Now, I was in a strange, unwelcoming place, feeling panic and loneliness settle over me like a heavy blanket.

Before the tears came, I texted our Cougar chat—my sisters, daughters, and niece. They all sympathized, sending heart emojis and telling me to hang in there. They tried to sound upbeat and encouraging, even though I could feel the worry behind their words. Then Mama Bel called me. I was so touched, especially since it was almost midnight. She knew I was being transferred to rehab and felt my pain because she knew rehab centers all too well. Her voice was soft but heavy with understanding, and for a moment, it felt like she was right there, holding my hand.

After we hung up, the weight of the day pressed down on me. I curled up as best I could, letting the quiet tears come. Hugging the heart pillow the hospital had given me, I cried myself to sleep, wishing I could rewind time and be back in my hospital room with my balloons, my nurses, and that strange but comforting sense of safety.

CHAPTER 34
BUSTIN' OUT OF REHAB

I woke early, my eyes swollen and sore from crying myself to sleep the night before. Checking my phone, I was flooded with messages and voicemails. Ashley had posted about the previous night being the hardest of her life, and her words had sparked an outpouring of love and support. Everyone, it seemed, was praying for me—and I was, too.

A nurse brought in breakfast, a sad plate that looked like it had been assembled by someone with a personal vendetta against food. I couldn't touch it. Ashley came in first thing in the morning but left again to make a few calls, promising to be back soon.

Around nine, she returned and told me someone would assess me around noon. She asked again about a private room, but there were none available.

"Go on with your day," I urged her. "There's nothing more you can do for now." She left reluctantly, promising to return before the assessment.

After she left, an attendant came in to take my vitals and pulled back the curtain separating me from my roommate. A wave of repulsion washed over me. The curtain was filthy, grimy, and in desperate need of a wash. I couldn't touch it. I was exposed, powerless, and trapped in a place that reeked of neglect and disgust.

I noticed my roommate, now dressed as if heading to church. She fussed with her wig in the mirror as an attendant came to say her ride was waiting. She looked friendlier than last night when she had barked at me about her dresser being off-limits.

Feeling brave or maybe just looking for a distraction, I decided to start a conversation. "Good morning. Going anywhere exciting?"

"Not at all," she muttered, "just a doctor's appointment."

I pushed on. "Still, must feel nice to get dressed up and leave for a bit. How long have you been here?"

"Two years," she replied. "I live here."

That opened the floodgates. She went on about the system failing her, the long wait for a better facility, and how the process was dragging on. I didn't mind; anything was better than staying on her bad side.

Before she left with the attendant, she turned to me. "Have a nice day," she said, then muttered under her breath, "So young... what's she doing here?"

I had to laugh at the irony. Here I was, a woman who still felt like there was so much left to do, yet in that moment I felt as if I had aged years. And there she was, saying I was so young to be in a place like this. Her words lingered long after she left. Maybe I didn't feel young, but the fact that she thought so was the reminder I needed. Maybe I still had time to turn things around.

When the attendant came to take away my untouched breakfast tray, I asked if I could finally get a shower. It had been almost three weeks, and I felt disgusting. She said she would check.

Not long after, another attendant appeared and asked, "Would you like a shower?"

"Yes, please!" I practically shouted, a wave of relief rushing through me.

She wheeled me down the hall to a door marked Showers. Inside, she helped me undress, then wrapped my chest in layer upon layer of what felt like industrial-strength plastic wrap, securing it with tape until I was practically shrink-wrapped. I couldn't help but laugh. I felt less like a patient and more like a UPS package ready to be shipped.

Once I was sealed in, she transferred me onto a rolling stool and wheeled me under the showerhead. When the water hit, warm, strong, and steady, I thought I had died and gone to heaven. I closed my eyes, letting the water pour over me, each drop washing away not just the grime but the feeling of being trapped in that place. For the first time in weeks, I felt human again. It wasn't just a shower. It was freedom, dignity, and a small piece of normalcy. Every drop of water felt like a miracle, a reminder of the balloons in my hospital room cheering me on, silent witnesses to my survival.

When the shower was over, I was dressed in a clean gown and wheeled back to my room. I checked my phone. Ashley had texted that she was on her way back. The staff would assess me to see how well I could walk with and without the walker and whether I could manage the toilet on my own. If I passed, I might be able to go home that very day. But they wouldn't discharge me unless someone was at home to care for me.

A shimmer of hope sparked in my chest, but it quickly faded. Ashley couldn't stay with me much longer. She had already been there for almost a month, and I hadn't been able to find anyone else to help. I called around, but with everyone having jobs and lives of their own, the chances were slim. When Ashley arrived, I confessed that I hadn't been able to find anyone who could spare that much time.

She smiled. "Don't worry," she said. "We've got it covered." She had already worked out a care rotation with the family. They would take turns coming to stay with me until I was strong enough to manage on my own.

While we waited for the staff to assess me, I practiced walking to the bathroom and back, testing myself with and without the walker. It was slow, but I was managing. Every step, though laborious, was a victory, like the balloons watching over me all those nights.

When the assessor arrived, I walked to the bathroom, sat on the toilet, then stood again as instructed. I then crossed the floor without the walker, inching my way forward one careful step at a time. They also had me walk up and down the hallway, slowly and deliberately, every step feeling heavier than the last. It wasn't pretty. I moved slower than a turtle, but I did it. Back in the room, we talked about the care plan. Ashley handed over the schedule, and the staff seemed satisfied with the arrangements.

Then came the words I had been waiting for. They would draw up my discharge papers. I was going home that day.

I could hardly believe it. After everything, after one miserable night in that dreary, unkempt place, I was finally being set free. When they handed me the discharge papers, Ashley and I exchanged a look, the kind that needed no words.

She wheeled me down the long corridor toward the front doors. The air felt lighter, fresher, full of possibility. As we approached the automatic doors and the afternoon sunlight spilled across my lap, I closed my eyes and let it wash over me. In that instant, the dreary, impersonal rehab facility fell away. I remembered my hospital room with its riot of balloons, each one a tiny guardian, each one a spark of hope and comfort. I had been trapped and scared, yet here I was, stepping out into sunlight, alive and free.

After everything, I wasn't just leaving a facility. I was stepping back into my life. Beneath the warmth, a faint chill lingered, a whisper of challenges still ahead, a reminder that some of my hardest struggles were waiting quietly in the shadows.

I was stepping back into my life, grateful and alive, yet beneath the relief, something heavy was stirring, patient and unresolved.

CHAPTER 35
THE COMFORT OF HOME

Coming home felt wonderful. The pugs were beside themselves with excitement, though we had to be careful they didn't jump near my chest. I clutched my heart pillow, which was now a part of me, a small comfort amid the lingering unease still stirring in my chest.

Upstairs in my bedroom, Ashley had set up a large playpen so the dogs could be close without climbing onto the bed. The rotation of caregivers ran smoothly. Ashley left the next day, and Kristin flew in to spend several days with me. When she left, Joji came next, followed by my sister-in-law, Ingrid, and my nephew, Joshua, who stayed a few weeks. My brother joined them later.

Ingrid transformed the downstairs area into her temporary office and filled the house with the comforting smell of her cooking. Every morning, she served me breakfast in bed, then helped me downstairs for lunch, where I could watch TV or sit in the backyard. Afterward, I'd head back upstairs for a nap. I was still on heavy medication, sleeping most of the day, but surrounded by care and love.

Manny even came to visit with his wife, Agnes. Our divorce had been amicable, and over the many years, we had managed to remain family—his and mine, all intertwined. His nieces, Marie and Polly, even drove in from Utah to see me. I felt truly blessed.

Then Thanksgiving came, and Ingrid prepared a feast. Ashley and her fiancé, Kris, drove out to spend the holiday with us. Rick even joined us for this special meal. We had a wonderful spread and so much to be thankful for, especially that my collapsed heart valve had been caught in time; otherwise, I wouldn't have been alive to celebrate.

The next day, Ashley and Kris returned home to San Diego, and the following day Jun, Ingrid, and Josh drove back to California after spending two weeks caring for me. By then, I was able to get around the house and cook my own meals. But suddenly, it was too quiet. Each morning, I woke feeling empty, going through some kind of withdrawal or simply adjusting to the silence. I was still weak, but I could drive short distances and had to be careful not to overexert myself.

As Christmas approached, I felt a deep yearning to spend it in California with my family. I had clearance from my doctor, though I still needed wheelchair assistance at the airports. I was genuinely excited and looking forward to every moment. I spent several wonderful days there, savoring time with everyone, and almost didn't want to return home. But I had to. I missed my fur babies too much.

I flew back home to Vegas two days after Christmas, still riding the high from spending the holiday with my family. Rick was kind enough to pick me up from the airport, and then we went to collect Rupert and Mona from the doggy hotel. Seeing them again was such a joy. I decided not to stay out there through New Year's, wanting a quiet celebration with just my pugs.

Returning to an almost empty house, just me and the dogs, was bittersweet. It felt a little sad after the bustle of family, yet there was also a sense of calm and relaxation. I was feeling a little stronger every day, able to take more steps on my own, and navigating the stairs was gradually getting easier. Although I still relied on the banister for support, I could feel real progress.

For a moment, I allowed myself to savor the quiet, the soft warmth of the sun through the windows, the little joys of home: a nuzzle from one of the pugs, the comfort of a blanket, the ordinary rhythm of daily life. I thought I was ready to move forward, to embrace the new year with gratitude and hope.

But that feeling of strength and calm didn't last long. Deep down, I couldn't ignore the subtle, nagging unease, a whisper that something wasn't quite right. The storm wasn't over. Vegas had its own plans, and the new year would bring an unexpected detour, one that would land me back in the hospital and test my body and my spirit in ways I hadn't anticipated.

CHAPTER 36
HAPPY NEW YEAR

On December 30, the day before New Year's Eve, I woke up feeling very strange—so strange it's hard to describe. I wasn't in pain beyond the normal post-surgical soreness, I just didn't feel right. At first, I brushed it off as fatigue from traveling, but as the day wore on, the unease only deepened.

By mid-afternoon, an unusual sensation stirred in my chest. It wasn't painful, just hollow, cavernous, an absence that pressed on me with every breath. My breathing grew irregular, and I found myself taking deep, involuntary breaths, not from climbing stairs, but from something else entirely. Something was wrong.

Now that I was cleared to drive short distances, I got in my car and headed to the ER at Summerlin Hospital. It was less than fifteen minutes away, but each moment in the car felt heavier than the last. My mind spiraled with what-ifs. What if it was serious? What if I didn't make it? Panic started to creep in as I gripped the steering wheel tighter, my palms slick with sweat and my heart hammering.

Every flash of sunlight off the windshield, every hum of passing tires, felt amplified, almost disorienting. The motion of the car pressed on my chest with every turn. And then the thought that terrified me most hit: what if this new heart valve was collapsing? After all, it was a pig's valve. My stomach knotted, my hands trembled, and I could barely focus on the road, willing myself to keep driving, keep breathing, and get to the hospital before it was too late.

Each passing second stretched into eternity. I kept repeating to myself: just get there, just get there, do not let it stop me. The hum of the tires, the rush of air through the vents, even faint music from the radio, all faded into the background, leaving only the pounding of my heart and the desperate rhythm of my own breath. Every intersection, every stoplight, every curve in the road was a challenge, and yet I pressed on, clinging to the hope that help was minutes away.

When I finally pulled into the ER parking lot, relief washed over me, but fear lingered. I knew from past experience that I didn't need to explain every detail to be seen. I just had to say I had chest pains and difficulty breathing. Clutching my chest and taking shallow, deliberate breaths, I walked in and told the triage nurse exactly that. Almost instantly, a wheelchair appeared, staff sprang into action, and I was whisked toward the care I desperately needed.

Once back, my vitals were taken immediately, followed quickly by an EKG. The staff had already looked up my records and knew about my recent heart valve replacement. They didn't share their findings, only that I needed to be admitted overnight for observation. A cardiologist wasn't available right away, but they brought me up to a room far better than the ER ward.

I was concerned about staying overnight, but if it was necessary, I accepted it. I called Rick and asked him to check Rupert and Mona into the doggy hotel, which he did without hesitation. He then came by to sit with me briefly, offering a small comfort amid the unease, though I could not shake the gnawing anxiety that had brought me here.

Shortly after he left, the cardiologist arrived. I disliked him immediately. Cold, distant, and lacking empathy, he made me feel as though I were wasting his time. My chest tightened as he asked clipped questions. He ordered an echocardiogram but said it wouldn't be done until the morning. He left almost as quickly as he arrived, and I tried to steady my breathing, but each beat of my heart echoed my fear.

The next morning, a technician performed the echo. The test itself took less than an hour, but I had to wait several more hours before the cardiologist returned, during which the hollow sensation in my chest seemed to grow heavier with every passing minute.

When he finally returned, he said I had pericardial effusion. I had to ask what it meant—fluid was building around my heart. When I asked what could be done, he simply said, "Nothing for now. We will just observe. You will stay another night so we can monitor you." Then he left. He didn't even stay long enough for questions, leaving me with fear and that hollow pressure pressing on me.

That day dragged slowly toward midnight. It was New Year's Eve, and instead of ringing in the new year with Rupert and Mona, I was in a hospital bed, hooked up to monitors. Missing the holiday pressed heavily on me. I tried distracting myself with social media and texting friends and family, but the disappointment lingered.

The hollow pressure persisted, a constant reminder that my heart and my plans were not entirely my own. Thoughts swirled in my mind, and one fear cut sharply through everything: here I was, fifty-seven years old—was it my time to go? I longed for the soft weight of my pugs, their warmth, steady breathing, and the simple joy of being home. Every beep of a monitor, every footstep in the hallway, made the longing ache more sharply.

Despite the fear, I reminded myself that I was being monitored, and the experts were keeping a close eye. Still, knowing I had to stay another night made the hours crawl. I closed my eyes, trying to summon calm, but sleep was uneasy, each breath a reminder that my body and heart needed more than rest.

The next day, the cardiologist never returned. By late afternoon, my patience had worn thin. I asked the nurses about my status, including if there was improvement, deterioration, or a plan. Nobody could give me a straight answer. By evening, it was clear I wasn't going anywhere, and still no doctor had checked in. All I could do was vent on social media, where friends sent advice, advocate contacts, and numbers for people familiar with the system who might help.

The nurses were kind and sympathetic, but powerless. They kept putting in requests for a doctor, and eventually one arrived. He asked a few basic questions, then reminded me I'd have to wait for the cardiologist before anything could move forward. The helplessness pressed down on me, and I felt trapped, lonely, and abandoned—like I was back at the rehab center all over again.

That night, I couldn't sleep. Just before midnight, IV lines trailing, I stood in front of the mirror. On impulse, I snapped a selfie with tired eyes, hospital gown, everything, and posted it on Facebook with a "Happy New Year" message. Every year, that photo appears in my memories, transporting me back to that hollow ache, the weight of uncertainty, and the desperate hope that things would improve.

I barely slept the next two nights, insomnia wrapping around me like a vice. I could have asked for something to help, but I didn't. Instead, I lay awake, thoughts spinning, wondering if this was my life now. In and out of hospitals, attached to machines, living in constant fear of what might go wrong next. The question lingered in the darkness, heavy and unsettling.

The next morning, I felt slightly better. The empty, weighty sensation faded, and my breathing was steady. For that reason, I assumed I would be discharged. But when the staff told me they wanted to keep me another night for observation, I felt crushed. Trapped. The hospital walls pressed in.

Rick came by again, bringing a brief sense of normalcy, but when he left, the silence pressed harder than ever. The TV was mounted too high to watch, leaving only my phone for distraction. I scrolled endlessly, texting, checking social media, anything to remind myself life outside still moved while mine felt paused.

I had closed out 2017 in this bed, and now I was beginning 2018 here, too. The thought chilled me. Was this an omen for the year to come?

At last, the next day, they discharged me. Relief washed over me the moment I walked through the front door. Rick had already picked up Rupert and Mona, who wagged their tails furiously as if they knew I needed them more than ever. I sank into the comfort of home, grateful, whispering silently, *Please let this be the last time.*

But deep down, I knew better. This was not the end, only the beginning.

CHAPTER 37
NIGHT TO SHINE

January came and went. Even so, although the physical aches were gone, I found myself sinking more and more often into a quiet, creeping sadness I couldn't explain. My body was recovering, growing stronger each day, but my mind and heart seemed to lag behind. Maybe that was why I had signed up with my church to volunteer for Tim Tebow's Foundation Night to Shine before my unexpected heart surgery. I needed something meaningful, a reason to step out of my own head and into someone else's world.

Tim Tebow's Foundation Night to Shine is an annual event for individuals aged fourteen and up to experience a prom-style night like no other. Each guest is treated like royalty: volunteers help with hair, makeup, and shoe shines; they are crowned kings and queens, then they ride a limo across the church campus to cheering paparazzi snapping photos as they make their entrance. Inside awaits dinner, dancing, and the joyful reminder that every person has dignity and worth.

The year before, I had volunteered at the thrift shop, sorting through donated dresses, suits, and accessories for the event. I loved helping guests find their perfect outfits and seeing their faces light up when everything came together. That excitement was priceless. I also worked the night of the event, helping with hair and makeup. It was such a moving experience that I decided, for the 2018 Night to Shine, I wanted to serve as a "buddy."

Buddies were paired with guests after they were dressed and crowned. Everyone was treated like a king or queen, spending the evening as their companion, riding the limo, walking the red carpet, and dancing together. When my application had been approved six months earlier, I was thrilled. As February approached, I realized the day was almost here.

By then, I was confident that I was well enough to keep my commitment. It would not be physically demanding, just an evening of joy, encouragement, and kindness. I could not wait.

When the day arrived, I was almost giddy getting ready. It felt like preparing for a prom of my own. I took extra care with my hair and makeup, slipped into a black dress, and after so long, felt glamorous again.

At the church, the energy was electric. Laughter, chatter, and music filled the air. After checking in, I joined the line of buddies waiting to be paired with our guests. Two lines faced each other, buddies on one side and guests on the other, each dressed to the nines, smiles radiant. None of us knew who we would be paired with until the organizers called us forward one by one. Each match was met with cheers and applause.

When I reached the front of the line, I spotted a young lady I had helped months earlier at the thrift store. I was thrilled, until someone stepped in and said she already had a reserved buddy. She was whisked away, and I felt a pang of disappointment.

Then I saw the next guest, a young man in a wheelchair. He appeared to have cerebral palsy and could not move himself. I hesitated, unsure if I had the strength to push him across campus, a block's distance, since we could not ride the limo. He was a big teenager, and without footrests, his feet dragged slightly as he was pushed. As we were introduced, I greeted him warmly, though he could not respond. His arms hung loosely in front of him. I whispered a quick prayer for strength.

Something seemed to take over as we moved across campus, perhaps the Holy Spirit, because a surge of energy carried me forward. The red carpet came into view. When it was our turn, I handed the announcer the card that was given to me. He read it aloud: "Please welcome Daniel!" The crowd, mostly volunteers acting as paparazzi, erupted with cheers and flashing cameras. I had not expected to feel so proud and uplifted.

Inside, the venue looked like a fairy tale. Every guest shone like a Cinderella or Cinderfella. The music was lively, the dance floor packed. I wheeled Daniel to a table for two, then made him a plate of pasta, potato salad, bread, and a cookie, plus water. He refused everything but the cookie, which he ate happily, then finished his water.

We sat listening to music until Daniel began making sounds, low groans that shifted into movement. His arms flailed, his body swayed. At first I panicked, thinking he might be in distress, but then I realized he was dancing. I wheeled him onto the floor, dancing beside him so he could see me. He twisted and swayed with pure joy, smiling the whole time. We stayed there until the last song.

When the evening ended, Daniel's caregiver arrived. I told her he had not eaten dinner, only the cookie. She laughed. "That's fine, he ate before coming." Then she encouraged him to say thank you. He tilted his head toward me and made soft groaning sounds, almost like crying. "He really took a liking to you, Miss Janette," she said.

As I left that night, I felt something awaken inside me. Strength, I realized, is not always physical. Sometimes it is measured by patience, heart, and the willingness to show up. I had walked in uncertain, and walked out grateful, proud, and deeply moved.

That night reminded me that life does not always unfold as planned. But when we open ourselves to the unexpected, extraordinary things can happen, moments that heal and remind us what truly matters. As I drove home smiling, replaying Daniel's joy in my mind, I realized something important: sometimes the very things we fear we cannot do are the moments that define us.

Still, as the night faded behind me, a quiet unease returned. Life had a way of testing me when I least expected it, and deep down, I knew another test was coming.

CHAPTER 38
TUG AT MY HEART

The Sunday after Night to Shine, I arrived at church early, as I often did. The joy from the previous week still lingered, warming me from within, though a trace of the quiet unease from that night remained. I felt good, grateful even, but still cautious, aware of how fragile my recovery was.

As I passed the volunteer desk, a familiar face greeted me warmly and mentioned they needed a few more volunteers upstairs to help with ushering and collecting donations. I glanced at the long staircase behind him. Steep, endless. I shook my head. I wasn't ready, or so I thought. But just as at Night to Shine, a quiet tug in my heart grew stronger until I could no longer ignore it. I stood, walked back to the desk, and said, "I'll do it." A mixture of anticipation and nervous energy coursed through me as I prepared to climb the stairs and serve.

The tasks themselves were simple: greeting guests, ushering, and collecting donations. Still, each step felt like a small victory. Everything went smoothly, and I left that service feeling a light, elated sort of joy.

Afterward, I indulged in my usual post-church ritual: sushi. Edamame, a rainbow roll, and unagi nigiri. I savored every bite, reflecting not just on the service, but on the year I had lived through. Everything I had endured—the fear, the heart surgery, the slow recovery—felt condensed into this quiet, contemplative moment. Then the realization came as clearly as the sunlight on the sushi counter. I was ready to be baptized.

I had been baptized as a baby in the Catholic Church, but this would be different. Now, I wanted it fully and intentionally, on my own terms. Growing up Catholic, mass had felt formal and distant, with priests chanting or reading from the Bible and little of it sinking in. The non-denominational church I had recently joined was alive and engaging. The pastor explained the Bible in a way that spoke to everyday life, and the worship music pulsed with energy. It captivated me.

I invited a few friends to witness both my service and baptism. Immediately after church, they handed me a T-shirt that read, "Have I got a story to tell you." I slipped it on and followed them to the outdoor fountain pond. It was beautiful, surprisingly large, with steps on either side. I was the first person to be baptized that day—April 1, Easter Sunday.

Stepping into the waist-high water, the gentle flow of the fountain surrounded me. I felt a surge of elation. Walking to the pastor, anticipation built in my chest. She asked why I wanted to be baptized, and I explained the tug in my heart. She asked if I was ready to receive Jesus Christ as my Savior, and I said, "Yes." With that, she gently dunked my head under the water.

When I emerged, cheers erupted. My friends beamed with love and support. I was flooded with pure, overwhelming joy. Standing there, dripping in sunlight, I reflected on how far I had come. Just months earlier, fear and uncertainty had defined my days. I had been vulnerable, limited, unsure if I would ever feel strong and whole again. Now, I was baptized on my own terms, fully present and fully alive.

That moment was not just about faith. It was about resilience, recovery, and reclaiming the joy and purpose of life. I realized that strength is not always physical. Sometimes it is measured by the heart, by patience, and by the willingness to show up fully for yourself and others.

Even as I left the pond, smiling and replaying the joy in my mind, a small, quiet thought whispered that life still had a way of testing me when I least expected it. The unease I had felt at Night to Shine had not completely vanished, but in that moment it did not matter. I had chosen life, chosen hope, and chosen myself.

CHAPTER 39
NO MORE SIS

After my baptism on Easter Sunday, I felt a renewed sense of clarity and purpose. The joy and elation from that day still lingered, but so did a quiet awareness that life would continue to test me in unexpected ways. It wasn't long before that awareness became tangible in my everyday interactions.

Rick had been there a lot for me since I moved to Vegas. He was always willing and available to help around the house, especially with the dogs when I was in and out of the hospital. He still called me "Sis," which I didn't mind. I welcomed it because it felt safe, like he understood our boundaries, and I had no romantic interest from my end. Yet, I later learned that others sometimes found it concerning. To them, Rick occasionally seemed possessive whenever he used the nickname. As time went on, I began to realize there were signs he might want—or hope for—something more.

I met many of the regulars at the Rocks Lounge, where Rick first brought me when I arrived. Some became friends, and I met others who eventually did as well. One of them was Jon, a big, burly bartender who was charming and had a way of making the ladies feel special. Jon and I would occasionally go out for sushi, just as friends enjoying a meal together, nothing more. But Rick was clearly bothered when Jon and I started talking more. He began giving sharp warnings, bad-mouthing Jon openly, insisting he was a player and claiming I would regret spending time with him. At the bar, he even complained that the wine glasses Jon served him smelled like a wet rag and often insisted on having them replaced.

What had once sounded like nitpicking now carried an edge of bitterness. Even during my work on Vegas on Air with my good friend Donny, I sensed Rick's jealousy. Donny helped me start my pole page on Facebook and even managed it with me. He had a girlfriend, whom Rick had met when she modeled for one of my fashion events, yet Rick still seemed unsettled whenever I mentioned Donny. The way he reacted to any man in my orbit hinted at something more than friendly concern.

One evening, while visiting Donny and his girlfriend, I got a heads-up about Rick. They had recently run into him at Red Rock. Rick approached to say hello but quickly began interrogating Donny about me: how we met, how long we'd known each other, and whether we had dated. Donny, leaning back in his chair, gestured with his hands, rolled his eyes, and recounted the encounter. Then, with that classic Italian flair in his gestures and accent, mimicking his own tone, he said in a firm, no-nonsense voice, "Rick, listen, none of that's your business. Back off, or you're gonna lose her as a friend, capisce?"

I felt relief and amusement. Someone had finally set boundaries for Rick. I could relax a little; someone had my back. Donny knew me well enough to know I would never tolerate being smothered by this kind of friendship.

But Rick didn't stop. Not long after my surgery, I began noticing his possessiveness more clearly. I limited my outings with him, but if I spoke with another man, Rick would butt in almost immediately, as if staking a claim. At home, I became careful not to ask for his help. The less time I spent with him, the harder he tried to convince me to get together. Eventually, I told him the truth: his persistence felt suffocating, and I needed space.

He didn't take it well. He reminded me of all the things he had done for me, which was a lot, and I thanked him sincerely. Then he started listing them, as if reading from a receipt: helping me move, carrying furniture, hanging paintings, setting up the TV. I reminded him that he had strongly encouraged me to move to Vegas in the first place. He had reassured me beforehand that he would handle all the handy work as a favor, which is why I felt comfortable making the move.

The part that bothered me most was that his girlfriend had already left for California by the time I moved. I had uprooted my life under the impression that the three of us would spend time together, when in reality it was just him. It felt less like generosity and more like manipulation.

He began texting and calling nonstop. I finally put the brakes on our interactions, thanking him for everything he had done while making it clear there was nothing more than friendship. He disagreed, insisting we had shared a lot together. I corrected him gently but firmly. I was grateful for his support, but only as a friend. We needed to cool things off.

Rick didn't like it. His calls and texts slowed but didn't stop, and when we did speak, there was always a trace of guilt-tripping. Subtle reminders of favors and assistance crept into every conversation, confirming that space was necessary. Eventually, I stopped responding.

Weeks passed with no contact, but I soon heard that he had been talking incessantly about me to others, describing our closeness as if I belonged to him, trying to make it seem as though we shared something exclusive. It was unsettling to realize that my absence did not stop his attention. It only intensified it.

Not long after, I stopped by Rocks Lounge alone and spotted my friends Mike and Lynn, a married couple, at the video poker machines. Mike always greeted me with a hug that lingered a little longer than usual. We shared an unspoken bond, having both undergone heart valve replacements, a connection rooted in survival and understanding. Every time Rick had witnessed those hugs in the past, he would roll his eyes and mutter insults.

While we caught up, a bartender leaned in and whispered that Rick was across the bar. I looked up and saw him glaring at us. Moments later, he stormed over, yelling at Mike, calling him a pervert, and creating a scene. Security moved in quickly, and Rick was escorted out. I later learned that Rick was 86'd from Rocks Lounge, permanently banned for his behavior.

Then came a long, tense text. Rick accused me of being unfair despite everything he had done. I calmly explained that I appreciated his help but was only interested in friendship. I was not obligated to be in a romantic relationship, and my feelings did not align with his assumptions.

Next, he demanded $3,000 for work around my house. I was stunned. I typed a firm response: I would reimburse legitimate expenses, but $3,000 was absurd. I wrote him a check for $800, leaving it at his house when I knew he wasn't home. Later, he thanked me, but I was irritated that he accepted any money at all. Those favors had never been transactional.

The texts continued, his tone swinging from pleading to obsessive. The constant pressure left me tense and unsure how to respond. Eventually, I turned to my friend Tim, someone who had earned my trust over time. He helped with house projects and provided support I could fully rely on. Over the years, we became very good friends and have stayed in close touch even to this day.

I stopped answering Rick completely. When necessary, I sent a final message stating I was not interested in a friendship or a relationship and that his behavior made me feel unsafe. I made it clear that further contact would result in legal action. At last, I could breathe, knowing I had claimed my space, my peace, and my life back.

With Rick finally out of my life, the relief was profound, but I knew that life's tests were not over. My victories in setting boundaries and reclaiming my space felt empowering. Yet my body reminded me that recovery was still fragile. Alongside the physical challenges, a quiet heaviness had begun to settle in my mind, a weight I could not yet name. Little did I know, the months ahead would bring new trials in both my health and my heart, testing my strength in ways I had yet to imagine.

CHAPTER 40
LEAVING LAS VEGAS

Spring came and went, and with it, Rick faded from my life. The texts and voicemails finally stopped. A few years later, he sent a brief hello. I replied politely, wished him well, and that was it. That was enough. Knowing he was no longer a threat gave me the closure I needed.

As summer approached, my focus returned to myself, but it was not easy. Healing from the valve replacement was slow. Heart palpitations struck without warning, sometimes sending me back to the hospital with fluid building around my heart. I was still weak, nowhere near ready for pole fitness or any kind of cardio. Some days I felt a spark of energy only to be taken down again by racing heartbeats, shortness of breath, and the simple struggle of climbing stairs. By then, I had learned to recognize when something could be managed at home and when it could not.

Because of that, I was not ready to work and could not keep my commitment with the aviation academy. I had been scheduled to start the previous October, but my heart valve collapsed just before then. They wished me a speedy recovery and assured me there would still be a place for me when I was ready. It stung. It was another reminder that my body now dictated the terms of my life. I felt frustration, longing, and grief. My recovery was not just about healing; it was a constant battle with my own body, a reminder that every step and every breath came with limits I could not ignore. Each day tested my patience, my spirit, and my resolve. Some days, it felt as though I was sinking deeper into the struggle rather than moving forward.

By late summer, when no real progress came, regret began to creep in. I started questioning my move to Nevada. All my family was in California. I was alone, still fragile, and nowhere near ready to work. I missed my girlfriends, their laughter, their comfort, the way we lifted each other up. Without them, the loneliness pressed harder. I had to put both Live for Chic and Live for Pole on hold. It was impossible to keep them going. The uncertainty gnawed at me. Would I ever get better?

I began sinking into a dark place, questioning everything. Some days I could not get out of bed. I cried for hours, my only comfort the steady warmth of Rupert and Mona curled beside me. The silence in my house felt heavier than usual, almost thick, as if the walls were holding their breath with me. I felt worn down, and even simple tasks felt impossible. I would sit on the edge of my bed, staring at the floor, trying to convince myself to move. The weight pressing on my chest only grew heavier.

It was the beginning of a darkness I did not yet understand, a slow unraveling that crept in quietly and wrapped itself around me before I realized what was happening. For the first time, I began to seriously entertain a thought that had been hovering at the edges of my mind. Ending it. Taking my own life. As a Christian, I knew it was considered a grave sin, something I had been taught never to contemplate. But in my darkest moments, I wondered if damnation could truly be worse than what I was living through. I felt as though I was already dying, my body failing me day by day, whether I chose the timing or not.

Even as those thoughts surfaced, there was one thing that held me here. Ashley's wedding. I wanted desperately to live long enough to see her walk down the aisle. I believed, with a quiet certainty, that death was coming for me soon regardless of my choices. Still, every night I prayed. I asked God for one thing only: to let me survive long enough to see my daughter get married.

That was when I discovered Devi Prayer. It became my ritual, my anchor. I would dim the lights until the walls blurred into shadow, light a candle, and sit cross-legged on the floor. I pressed play and let the chant fill the room, looping it for hours until time seemed to dissolve. The ancient Sanskrit verses honoring the Divine Mother wrapped around me like a veil.

I rocked gently as the music swelled, tears falling freely. Sometimes I felt a strange warmth, as if the sound itself was loosening something knotted deep inside me. When the music stopped, silence rushed back in, heavy and suffocating. Still, the ritual gave me just enough strength to keep breathing.

By fall, it was clear I would not be able to work anytime soon. My move to Vegas had turned into a cycle of hospitals, fear, and endless medical bills. My savings drained as quickly as my energy. My family began urging me to move back to California, worried about me being alone. Their concern echoed what I already knew. I was falling apart.

Ashley suggested I move in with her and Kris in San Diego and help with their wedding planning. It should have sounded like hope, but instead it felt like failure. Leaving Vegas meant admitting defeat, that I was too sick, too weak, too broken to make it on my own. I had told myself it was Las Vegas or bust, and now the city that once symbolized freedom had worn me down.

I drifted in and out of darkness. The idea of moving only deepened my depression. I had to sell all my furniture and downsize everything I owned until it felt like dismantling my life piece by piece. My wardrobe had once been my signature, rows of designer shoes, handbags, and accessories that told my story. Now I photographed them, posted them online, and watched strangers carry them away. Deep down, I believed I would not live much longer. Selling it all felt like preparing for the end.

Letting go was agony. Every item held a piece of who I had been, the woman who dressed with intention, took pride in details, and stepped into the world with purpose. That woman felt gone. Packing felt like putting her away, box by box.

It took about two months to sell what I could. I still had several boxes of Live for Pole and Live for Chic merchandise. Tim let me store them in his garage until the next Pole Expo. I planned to sell everything at clearance prices, just to close that chapter as well.

Ashley, Kris, and his friend came to Vegas with a small U-Haul. They loaded what they could, then Ashley filled my SUV with the rest, along with Rupert and Mona. As we drove away, I turned to look back at the house one last time. Nostalgia and unease welled up, tears spilling as I wondered whether moving there had been a mistake. Would my heart have failed if I had stayed in California? The questions had no answers.

Exactly two years had passed since I first left California on October 19, 2016. Back then, I had been filled with excitement and hope, eager to see what Las Vegas had in store for me. The city felt like a blank canvas, bursting with opportunity. I imagined the life I would build, the adventures I would have, the independence I would claim.

One year later, on October 19, 2017, that excitement had collapsed. I had faced the terrifying reality of emergency open-heart surgery, the kind I would not have survived without immediate intervention. Fear took over. Every heartbeat felt fragile. The city that once promised possibility had become a place filled with reminders of my vulnerability.

Now, on October 21, 2018, I was returning home. I left behind a city that had offered both brief exhilaration and relentless fear. I carried the lessons of survival, the weight of what I had endured, and the heavy presence of depression that had followed me through those months. Las Vegas had tested me in ways I never anticipated, but California offered the possibility of stability, healing, and perhaps a path forward, even if the journey would be slow.

Yet even as I left, the darkness came with me. My body was weak, my heart unpredictable, and my mind heavy with despair. I had survived one storm, but another, quieter one still raged inside me.

CHAPTER 41
UNPACKING SHADOWS

When we arrived at Ashley and Kris's two-bedroom house, with a small bonus room up a narrow flight of stairs, I was genuinely moved. Ashley had decorated my room to be cozy and welcoming, even building a futon bed just for me. At first, I felt a small glimmer of hope in the midst of all the change.

But as we began unloading my belongings into my room and the bonus room, boxes stacked high and spilling over, the space Ashley had created quickly felt crowded and chaotic. I could not believe I was going from living in spacious homes for so long, just me, Rupert, and Mona, to this tiny room. The weight of my past, my independence, the life I had built, and the routines that had defined me seemed to fade with every box we carried upstairs. Depression settled heavily on my chest, dark and unrelenting, and once again, thoughts of hopelessness and escape returned.

Their house was cute, but realistically, it was too small for three people. Ashley and Kris decided to start looking for something bigger, especially since they were planning to start a family. Eventually, they bought a house that would serve all of us better. The garage had been converted into a separate living area with a living room, bathroom, and two small bedrooms. I would have my own space downstairs with a private entrance, giving us privacy while still being close enough to feel connected.

Even with the new space, the darkness returned. I often retreated into my room, dimmed the lights, and let the silence press in until it felt suffocating. Thoughts of inadequacy, loneliness, and mortality lingered constantly, whispering that I might never fully recover, that I would never regain the independence I once had or find my footing again. The fear sat heavy in my chest, quiet but relentless.

Some days I woke feeling almost normal, even a little hopeful. Then, without warning, the darkness crept back in, slow and uninvited, until I found myself trapped once again in that same suffocating place.

CHAPTER 42
WATCHING HER GLOW

Even as we moved forward into wedding plans and celebrations, the darkness did not stay behind. On the surface, everything looked joyful. And in small moments, it was. But beneath the smiles and laughter, that familiar cloud lingered, whispering doubts and fears I could not shake.

For the wedding weekend, we rented a large Airbnb near the venue. My sisters and their families stayed there, along with Kristin, Ashley, and me. The night before the wedding, we held a large rehearsal dinner with immediate family and out-of-town relatives. Laughter bounced off the walls, and the rich aroma of catered Persian food filled every corner. Everyone else seemed fully present, gliding through the evening with ease. I felt like I was behind a pane of glass, watching a life I used to know but could no longer reach.

I had made a generous batch of lumpia and fried them carefully outside in the air fryer, hoping the familiar routine would steady me. My hands trembled anyway. Every sizzle of oil, every pop and hiss felt amplified, echoing my restless heartbeat. My thoughts spiraled toward the future, my health, my place in the world. Even surrounded by family, I felt isolated, trapped inside my own head, a silent observer as life continued forward without me.

The next morning, everyone woke early. Ashley, Kristin, my two sisters, and my niece headed to the venue to have their hair and makeup professionally done. I stayed behind. I wished I could join them, but I was pinching pennies and could not justify the expense. I tried to get myself wedding-ready on my own. The false eyelashes refused to cooperate, my hair would not behave, and frustration slowly settled into a heavy sadness that crept in quietly and refused to let go.

Eventually, I pulled my hair into a messy bun and got dressed. When I arrived at the venue, the girls were glowing. Kristin noticed my unruly hair and gently fussed with it, offering a few small adjustments with quiet care. Watching Ashley laugh with her bridesmaids, sipping champagne and glowing from the inside out, I felt genuine joy for her, even as a flutter in my stomach reminded me how fragile those calm moments were.

During the reception, I offered grace, savored the food, and even smiled without forcing it. Bel, my dear friend, was my plus one, and it meant everything that she had driven all the way from Northern California just to be there. The wedding was everything Ashley had dreamed of, and witnessing her happiness lifted my heart, if only briefly. Still, beneath the smiles, a tightness curled in my chest and the flutter in my stomach grew stronger, a quiet warning that the darkness was waiting. Every laugh and cheer felt slightly out of reach, and I could sense the calm slipping away, soon to be replaced by a storm I could not yet see.

CHAPTER 43
CUPS AND CRIES

The next morning, reality came crashing back. Checkout day at the Airbnb was pure chaos. Half-empty wine glasses sat on every surface, dishes filled the sink, and garment bags were scattered everywhere. We had to pack, clean, and restore order before noon. In the middle of the scramble, someone noticed about thirty white chairs stacked in the backyard—the rental chairs from the rehearsal dinner. My stomach dropped. I suddenly remembered I had volunteered to return them, along with collecting all the leftover drinks from the venue, and it all had to be done by 11:00 a.m. The clock was already mocking me.

I recruited Kristin's boyfriend, Ryan, as my sidekick, and we loaded the car like a moving truck, racing against both the heat and the time. By the time we pulled up at the venue at 11:05, the sun was relentless, ninety-five degrees and climbing. We unloaded the chairs, packed the leftover beverages into the car, and I was soaked. Sweat plastered my hair to my face and clung to my skin.

Cindi, Kris's mother, was hosting an afternoon tea party for the same group who had attended the rehearsal dinner. It was a large gathering, and everyone had been encouraged to dress in tea party attire. Once we finished at the venue, we drove straight to Cindi's house. I was so exhausted and overheated that I did not even consider changing into a tea dress. I stayed in my shorts and T-shirt.

Walking through the door felt surreal. Men wore crisp suspenders. Women floated by in floral dresses and wide-brimmed hats. The entire room looked like it belonged in a magazine spread. And there I was, the mother of the bride, sweaty, disheveled, and painfully out of place.

The shame hit first. Then the tears.

I slipped into the kitchen and began sobbing uncontrollably. The crying would not stop. It shook me from the inside out, deep and relentless. Every few moments, someone quietly peeked in or asked what was wrong. Their voices were soft and kind, but I could not respond. No words came. My head spun, disconnected from my body, while my heart raced wildly. It felt as if I were slipping away, drowning in exhaustion and fear, powerless to stop it.

That was when my sister Jane rushed in. Along with her husband John and my niece, they each took hold of me, guiding me out of the house quietly but firmly. As we drove away, I stared out the window, trembling. I did not understand what had just happened. I only knew I needed to be somewhere safe, away from everyone's eyes.

When we got home, I lay down for a short nap. When I woke, I felt slightly better, though still fragile. My niece Erika and her husband Justin, along with Jane and John and their two sons, suggested we go out for burgers. Over dinner, the conversation eventually turned to what had happened. No one knew about the darkness I had been battling, so we landed on a reasonable explanation. It must have been the heat, the exhaustion, the stress. It made sense to them. Deep down, I knew it was more than that, but I stayed quiet.

Everyone could tell I was not myself. Kristin even postponed her flight back to the Bay Area so she could stay with me a few extra days. That night, the darkness returned in full force. I did not tell anyone. I did not want to alarm them again. I went to bed early, hoping sleep would wash it away.

It did not.

The next morning, the heaviness was still there, thick and suffocating. Jane and her family were heading to the beach and invited me to come along. I declined at first. I did not have the strength to pretend I was fine. A little while later, my nephews JR and Brenden came into my room.

"Please, Auntie Janette," they begged. "Come to the beach with us."

How could I refuse? These were the boys who had been so sad when I moved out earlier than planned, the ones I already felt I had disappointed. I loved them too much to say no again. I pushed myself up, got ready, and went with them.

Kristin joined us too, and to my surprise, we had a wonderful time. The salty air, the sound of the waves, and my nephews' laughter lifted me, even if only temporarily. For a few hours, the darkness loosened its grip.

I held onto that light for the rest of their stay. Surrounded by family and love, I could almost believe I was okay. But when they left, the silence returned, slow and suffocating, and once again, I found myself facing the shadows alone.

CHAPTER 44
STROKE OF DARKNESS

After the wedding weekend ended and everyone returned to their lives, I could no longer tell myself that what happened at Cindi's house was just heat or exhaustion. Something in me knew it was a warning, even if I did not yet understand what it meant. Something was wrong. My body kept insisting on it, even when I tried not to listen.

When I arrived in San Diego, one of the first things I did was find a doctor, a general physician. I liked her immediately. She seemed to genuinely care and never made me feel rushed. At first, I saw her every month because of the condition I was in. I gave her my full medical history, and she referred me to a cardiologist. Keeping close watch on my heart was essential. I also confided in her about the depression that had been weighing me down. She listened without judgment and referred me to a psychologist I began seeing weekly.

Even with all that support, I was not getting better. I was weak, constantly sick, and bone tired all the time. No matter what we tried, nothing added up. After endless blood tests and screenings for what felt like everything imaginable, the conclusion landed on some kind of autoimmune disease. Of course it did. That is what they call it when they cannot figure out what is wrong. Another vague label. Another weight added to my shoulders.

It fed directly into my depression. Most mornings I woke already exhausted, as though I had not slept at all. On better days, I might feel okay for a short while, only to be blindsided by sudden fatigue, sadness, and tears I could not control.

The uncertainty consumed me. I never knew how I would feel from one day to the next. Some mornings I woke hoping today might be different, only to crash hours later, my body betraying me again. Other days I opened my eyes already heavy, already dreading the effort of existing. The sadness came in waves I could not stop, sudden floods of tears that left me gasping.

Then came the thoughts I feared most. On my darkest days, I wondered again if life was even worth continuing. I began to believe maybe I was not meant to survive all of this, that my body breaking down was a sign it was time to let go. I carried a deep, persistent guilt I could not fully explain, as if I had done something wrong simply by still being here, as if happiness was something I no longer deserved. I never told anyone how deep my despair went or how often I found myself contemplating slipping quietly out of this world. The truth was, I no longer saw a future. I could not imagine one. All I could see was endless exhaustion, endless sadness, and the terrifying idea that there might be only one way to make it stop.

In those moments, I returned to the same ritual I had clung to in Vegas. I dimmed the lights, sat cross-legged on the floor, lit a candle, and played the Devi Prayer on repeat, twenty minutes at a time. The haunting chant, meant to honor the goddess, became something else entirely. I was not praying. I was surrendering, letting the sound carry my grief. I rocked back and forth as the voices filled the room, tears streaming down my face. It was my comfort and my release, the one place where I allowed myself to completely fall apart.

I became skilled at hiding my depression from everyone, even after my breakdown at Cindi's house the day after the wedding. But there was no hiding my physical symptoms. They exposed me again and again, reminding me and everyone around me that something was very wrong. The heart palpitations came without warning, forcing me to stop whatever I was doing and sit down until they passed. Sometimes they lasted minutes. Other times they stretched into hours, each beat pounding so violently I wondered if my heart might burst.

About a week after the wedding, my heart rate shot up to nearly two hundred. It felt as though my chest would explode, and Ashley rushed me to the ER. The doctors brought it down quickly, then casually sent me home with a few tips for next time, as if next time were not a terrifying thought.

A week later, it happened again. I was out running errands when the morning began to unravel. By late morning, a strange headache began pressing down on me, thick and heavy. It was not a normal headache, and it was not a migraine. It felt foreign. Wrong. As the hours passed, it sharpened, spreading through my skull like a gathering storm. By early afternoon, the pain radiated, my chest tightened, and my heart once again spiraled into chaotic palpitations.

As I walked out of CVS, I found myself facing the same hospital I had visited just a week before. It felt almost like fate. I thought, *What the heck, I am right here. If this is my heart valve again, I cannot ignore it.* Fear made the decision for me.

I drove across the street and walked into the ER. By then, my introduction had become automatic. My chest hurts. I am having trouble breathing. I am having heart palpitations. I did not mention the headache. Compared to my heart, it felt secondary.

Within minutes, they took me to the back, put me on oxygen, and ran an EKG. My heart rate came down, the lines on the screen steadying. The doctor reassured me the EKG was normal and that my heart sounded fine. Fine, even though I did not feel fine at all. Once the immediate danger passed, they wheeled me back into the waiting room, as though the urgency had evaporated.

About an hour later, they brought me back again. This time, they handed me a gown and placed me in a bed in the communal ER, separated from strangers by thin curtains that did little to muffle groans, monitors, cries, and muffled conversations. They ran through my vitals again, repeating the same routine.

When a doctor finally came in, I explained that although my heart rhythm had stabilized, my chest still felt tight, as if bracing for another attack. I also mentioned the headache, now impossible to ignore. She listened carefully and told me they wanted to keep me overnight until a cardiologist could see me in the morning.

Frustration set in immediately. Why was it that every time I landed in the ER, there was never a cardiologist available? Were heart issues not supposed to be emergencies? My mind drifted to *Grey's Anatomy*, where teams of specialists rushed in with urgency. Real life felt very different. Hurry up and wait, except it was my life on the line.

I called Ashley and told her what was happening and that I needed to stay overnight for observation. She came by after work and sat with me for a while. I was grateful, but I could not shake the feeling that I was becoming a burden.

The next morning, I did not feel much different, except for the strange, off sensation in my head. Not pain exactly, just wrong. They told me my heart was fine despite the tightness in my chest. I insisted something was being missed, and finally, the doctor agreed to order an MRI of my brain.

I warned her that I was claustrophobic and would likely panic without a sedative. Years earlier, during my first MRI, I had screamed and slammed the emergency button before it even began.

This time, they gave me Ativan through an IV. I felt my body loosen, the tight knots of fear dissolving. I even joked with the attendant as he wheeled me down the hall, making him laugh. Sliding into the capsule did not bother me. When the loud rhythmic pounding started, I imagined I was at a concert. The vibrations felt almost musical. By the end, I was oddly disappointed when it was over.

Later that afternoon, long after the Ativan wore off, I was still lying in the communal ER. Patients came and went all day, some moaning softly, others crying out in pain. Every sound pierced me. I wanted answers. What was causing these headaches, this heaviness, this steady unraveling of my body?

The doctor who ordered the MRI had already left for the day, leaving me in limbo once again. No instructions. No plan. Just waiting.

Late in the day, a male doctor pulled back the curtain and introduced himself as a neurologist. He said he wanted to discuss my MRI results. My heart skipped. Results meant they had found something.

His words knocked the breath out of me.

He told me the MRI showed I had suffered a stroke about two weeks earlier.

I froze. A stroke. It came out of nowhere. A chill spread through me, fear flooding my chest.

The neurologist asked if I had noticed any symptoms at the time, numbness, slurred speech, weakness on one side. I shook my head. None of that. Then I remembered the strange headaches, the ones that began right after the wedding. And suddenly it clicked.

The tea party.

The day after Ashley's wedding.

That moment at Cindi's house when I broke down, sobbing uncontrollably, unable to explain why, feeling detached from my own body. I told him about it. He nodded and explained that sudden, uncontrollable crying can be a sign of a stroke. It is called pseudobulbar affect, or PBA, and it happens when areas of the brain that regulate emotions are damaged.

I was stunned. What I thought had been exhaustion or stress was actually a stroke. A stroke the very next day after Ashley's wedding. My mind reeled, but one thought broke through the fear. Thank God it did not happen on her wedding day.

I asked, my voice trembling, whether PBA was permanent. He reassured me that in many cases it was not. As he spoke, my thoughts wandered. Was this connected to the depression I had been fighting for so long? For a brief moment, I wondered if this was the missing piece.

Then I knew better.

The darkness had already followed me from Vegas.

This was something else.

Something new.

CHAPTER 45
QUIET COLLAPSE

Physically, I was spared. Emotionally, I was not. I was fortunate that I did not suffer any major residuals from the stroke. The only thing I noticed afterward was that my short-term memory did not feel as sharp as it used to be, although I sometimes wondered if that was just age creeping up on me.

Even with that small relief, I could not shake the weight pressing on me. I was seeing my psychologist weekly and then a psychiatrist, too. They both reminded me that once you have had a stroke, the risk of another is higher. They warned me that depression and stress could be dangerous because both could raise my blood pressure. Their concern was real, and I appreciated it, but nothing inside me felt any different. If anything, I had fallen even deeper into the shadows since the stroke.

The guilt I carried grew heavier every day. My mind circled back to my childhood, to how small and irrelevant I often felt from the teasing at school and at home. I wondered if all of this was some kind of punishment. Maybe it was karma. Maybe it was because I moved out of the house at eighteen against my parents' wishes. Or because I divorced Manny, the perfect husband and the perfect father. Maybe I had been selfish for wanting out, for not being the wife he deserved. Maybe this was what I deserved.

And then there were the kidnappings. Some part of me still believed I must have done something to cause them, that I put myself in the wrong places or trusted the wrong people, that somehow I brought them on myself. Both of those experiences lingered in me like fresh bruises, adding to the endless layers of guilt I already carried.

The more I thought about everything, the more convinced I became that all the pain and chaos in my life was my fault. I felt like a burden to everyone around me, a constant source of worry and exhaustion. It felt like I was always in and out of hospitals, always needing help. There were still days when I secretly wished I would not wake up in the morning, that maybe the pain, mine and theirs, would finally stop.

Now, alongside my general physician, my cardiologist, my psychologist, and my psychiatrist, I had added a neurologist to the list. It almost sounded comical when I listed them out, like I was a project being managed by a committee. But it was not funny. It was exhausting. Sometimes just seeing all their names in my planner made me want to give up.

Life became a revolving door of medical offices. Every week I was either sitting on a couch, lying on an exam table, or staring at a waiting-room wall covered with faded health posters. Sometimes I wondered if my full-time job was being a patient. But it was the waiting that wore me down the most. Waiting for answers. Waiting for results. Waiting to find out whether my brain, my heart, or my mind would betray me next. The waiting fed my depression like gasoline on a fire.

Some mornings I woke up thinking maybe today would be different, only to have the heaviness return by afternoon, leaving me in tears I could not explain. I wanted to believe I could climb out of the hole, but there were days I did not even want to. There were days when the idea of disappearing, of not having to fight anymore, felt more comforting than frightening.

My daughters did not know the full extent of my depression, but they knew I was lonely. I had no friends. I never had the chance to make any in my condition. They kept suggesting I try to meet people, make new connections. Even my psychologist encouraged it. But I did not know anyone in San Diego. I remembered how easy it had once felt when we formed the GF Club, how strangers from Craigslist became family overnight. Making friends used to feel effortless. Now I doubted Craigslist even served that purpose anymore. I scoured the internet for any way to bring some life back into my world. I tried a few Meetup groups and attended a couple of events, but nothing clicked. No spark.

And then the world shut down. COVID-19 arrived like a wave and swallowed everything. Schools closed, offices went remote, businesses shut their doors. Everyone retreated behind screens. The world outside grew colder and more distant, and my depression seeped even deeper into my bones. I still kept up with my doctor appointments, holding onto whatever thread of stability I could, but as the darkness crept into everyone else's world, mine sank even further. As the months dragged on, the days became indistinguishable from one another. Morning, afternoon, night. Everything blurred into the same dull gray. I was not fighting anymore. I was not even pretending to. I went to my appointments because it was routine, because it was expected, because not going would only create more questions I did not have the energy to answer.

Inside, I felt empty. Not angry, not panicked, not even sad. Just finished. Something in me had quietly shut down, and nothing seemed capable of bringing it back. I stopped imagining a future. I stopped wanting one. Waking up felt like an inconvenience, another day I had to get through for everyone else. I was suspended in a place with no color, no sound, no direction. A place where surviving felt like the loneliest kind of punishment.

And then, even that small comfort was taken from me.

She was the last of my dogs, my little family. Rupert had passed the year before, and now Mona was joining him. They had been my life partners for almost fourteen years, loyal and constant through every heartbreak, every move, every long night I spent crying. Those two dogs had been with me longer than any man, longer than my marriage. Losing them felt like losing the last bit of unconditional love I had left in my life.

The silence in the house afterward was unbearable. No soft footsteps padding behind me, no snoring at the foot of my bed, no one waiting for me to come home. The emptiness swallowed me whole, and I cried until I could not anymore.

And that was where I stayed, disappearing a little more each day, convinced that nothing was ever going to get better.

CHAPTER 46
LEONIE

A couple of years went by, and the darkness followed me like a shadow I could not shake. Then, just as another year was drawing to a close, a tiny spark of life pierced through the gloom. Ashley and Kris announced they were having a baby.

For a moment, I felt a flutter of joy I had not known in months, a lightness I was not used to. But alongside the happiness, a quiet apprehension settled in. Could I allow myself to feel hope, even briefly, without the weight of my own struggles dragging it down? Even as I celebrated with them, a part of me remained bound to the shadows, watching and waiting, unsure if this new chapter could really bring any lasting warmth.

As the news settled in, I found myself drawn into their excitement: nursery ideas, baby names, tiny outfits, the endless imagining of what life would be like with a little one. I wanted to feel fully present, to share in the joy, but the darkness lingered at the edges of my mind. Some days I could laugh and help plan, but other days even the thought of holding a newborn felt overwhelming. I worried about my own fragility, my health, my depression, the shadows that never seemed to leave. Could I be a source of strength for them, or would I crumble and cast my gloom onto this bright new life?

Despite my fears, I could not help but be drawn to the wonder of it all. I watched Ashley's belly grow, her excitement radiating like a beacon, and for fleeting moments, I allowed myself to imagine a life unclouded by my own despair. I felt protective, not just of the baby, but of Ashley and Kris, wanting to be there fully for them, even if I still struggled to be fully there for myself.

The months passed slowly, marked by doctor's appointments, ultrasound images, and the quiet rhythm of anticipation. With every kick, every little hiccup from the baby, I felt a strange mixture of awe and unease. I was awed by the miracle unfolding before me, uneasy that my own body and mind were still delicate, still unpredictable. Yet in those moments, a delicate thread of hope began to form, weaving through the shadows that had defined my life for so long.

As Ashley's pregnancy progressed, I began to feel a quiet flicker of hope inside me. It was not an instant transformation or a grand revelation, just a subtle, growing sense that maybe, just maybe, life still had moments worth holding on for. Every time Ashley called me into her room to feel the baby kick, I pressed my hand gently against her belly. That faint flutter beneath my palm stopped me cold. That tiny heartbeat, steady, strong, alive, seemed to echo somewhere deep in my own chest, reminding me that I was still here too.

And then, gradually, something started to come alive inside me. I realized, with startling clarity, that I wanted to live. I wanted to get healthy. I wanted to look forward to each day, to experience more than just surviving. I wanted to embrace life, to give and receive love, to reconnect with joy in any form it could take. I started praying like I never had before, speaking to God with raw honesty. I asked Him to restore faith in me, to help me find the strength I had lost, and promised that whatever He had in store, I would accept it. But if I had a choice, I chose life.

There were still days when the darkness returned, when I retreated into my room and the silence wrapped around me like a thick fog. But even then, the thought of that baby, of Ashley becoming a mother, of me becoming a grandmother, kept glimmering in the back of my mind like a tiny candle refusing to go out. At that point, I was determined to live. I fought the darkness with everything I had, holding on to that fragile light, and I never stopped praying, calling on God for strength, guidance, and the courage to keep moving forward.

Then, on August 22, 2021, my granddaughter was born, a tiny, perfect light piercing through all the darkness. They named her Leonie, after my mother, Leonisa. The moment I saw her, something inside me awakened. Holding her for the first time, I felt a warmth I had not known in years, soft, tender, but real. It was as if all the love I had lost had quietly returned, bundled in a little blanket, breathing softly against my chest. That quiet prayer I had begun had become a refuge, a bridge to hope, and a reminder that even in the shadows, light could still be found.

Finally, I allowed myself to believe life could be beautiful again.

CHAPTER 47
FIREWALKER

Choosing life did not mean the darkness disappeared overnight. Even after Leonie's arrival, the shadows lingered, whispering doubts and fears, testing my resolve. But I had made a decision. I wanted to live, truly live, and I clung to that determination as I searched for ways to reclaim my strength and my joy.

A few years after the first kidnapping, Joji had encouraged me to attend a Tony Robbins event called *Unleash the Power Within*, best known for its "Walking on Fire" experience. The timing could not have been better. I have to admit it helped me more than I expected, and I carried much of what I learned there into the early years of my healing.

Walking across burning hot coals was meant to be a metaphor for fear and self-limitation, but it became something much deeper for me. With my eyes closed, I pictured myself stepping through the fire, not just once, but every time I had survived something I thought would break me. The shift in my attitude was immediate. I felt energized, grounded, and strong again.

I had loved it so much that I began returning to the events as a volunteer. I staffed them for years in different roles. I started with registration, then became an usher, and eventually guided people as they walked the fire. Every time I returned, I felt that familiar rush. By the end, I had volunteered close to a dozen times.

The last event I staffed is the one I remember the most. It took place only a few months before my open-heart surgery. That weekend, I worked on the Fire Team. We swept the grounds, laid out sod, assembled wheelbarrows, and built the fire from chopped wood. Once the fire was ready, we took turns, two of us at a time, moving in close. One person pushed the wheelbarrow toward the flames while the other shoveled burning coals into it. We repeated this over and over until the heat wrapped around us like a wall.

After many rounds, I felt my body giving out. The heat was overwhelming, and my legs wobbled beneath me. I finally had to stop shoveling and shouted, "I can't shovel anymore!"

My partner's voice rang out repeatedly, loud and steady: "Come on, girl, you got this."

Somehow I found the strength to continue, and I completed all twelve shovelfuls. As he wheeled the barrel of coals back to our lane, I led the way, arms raised, calling out, "Hot coals coming through." I still get a rush when I think about it and hear those words echo in my memory. Of all the positions I held as a volunteer, that one was my favorite.

Six months later, my heart valve collapsed. Healing was difficult, and the depression that followed nearly swallowed me. It felt as if everything in my world was falling apart. I tried again and again to lean on Tony's teachings and repeat the motivating words that once fueled me, but in that darkness nothing reached me.

I still value everything I learned at those events. I draw on many of the lessons daily. But in the end, something else was what truly woke me up and reminded me that life was still worth living.

Even after all the lessons from walking through fire, life continued to test me. The darkness lingered, heavy and uninvited, but it no longer had the power to consume me completely. I held on to whatever small moments of light I could find, reminders that there was still something worth staying for. And just when I believed I had little left to hope for, life offered me a new reason to lift my head, a gentle glow that grew into a light I never expected.

CHAPTER 48

HOW LEONIE SAVED ME: LIFE, LAUGHTER, AND DANCE

It was a blessing to have Leonie enter our lives during COVID, when the world outside had gone still and silent. While everything seemed frozen, she gave my life motion again. Being cooped up at home no longer felt lonely. Each morning, I had a reason to rise: to hold her, feed her, watch her smile, and see the world fresh through her tiny eyes. Kris and Ashley worked from home like most of the world then, so my days revolved around caring for Leonie and settling into my new role as Grandma.

Her presence was quietly transformative. The way her tiny fingers curled around mine or how her laughter filled the house like sunlight reached parts of me that had long been shadowed. It was more than joy; it was redemption. She reminded me that love could still grow, even amid fear and isolation.

Slowly, I began to heal, both mentally and physically. The fatigue that had clung to me like a second skin started to lift. I stopped getting sick constantly, and for the first time in years, I felt strong again. I had energy, purpose, and reasons to smile. My psychiatrist gradually weaned me off antidepressants, and my sessions with my psychologist became less frequent, first every two months, then only as needed.

Ashley noticed I was coming back to life and bought me a five-class pass for a dance studio called Madhouse Dance in San Diego, thinking it was a pole fitness studio. I had already decided to start living again, so I was excited. When I booked my first class, I discovered there was no pole dancing, but they did offer a variety of dance classes, so I signed up for a Dance Cardio class. I was slightly disappointed but went anyway, and I'm so glad I did.

The studio had three rows of eight spots each for students to choose from. As a newcomer, I naturally picked a spot in the back row, keeping some distance from the instructor and the mirror. I wasn't ready to watch myself dancing offbeat yet. Once the music started, I found myself moving along, wishing I were closer to the front so I could see the instructor's moves more clearly. By my second visit, I arrived early to grab a front-row spot right by the instructor so I could follow every move. I have done that ever since. I never imagined Dance Cardio could work out every single muscle in my body. The workout was intense, engaging every muscle with hip-hop moves and plenty of butt-twerking. It was even better for me than pole fitness because there was no bruising. I was addicted. I went three to four times a week, always arriving early for the front row. I still dance with a lack of rhythm, and I still cannot twerk, but I dance anyway.

It felt like waking up after a long sleep. The world hadn't changed, but I had. I could laugh without forcing it. I could breathe without the weight pressing down on my chest. I made a conscious decision to heal, to truly live again. I even revisited some of Tony Robbins' teachings, using mindset exercises, visualization, and firewalking imagery.

I remembered volunteering on the Fire Team, shoveling burning coals until my legs wobbled and my body begged me to stop. I had felt like giving up. I realized then that the lesson was never about enduring fire on the ground—it was about finding the fire within, summoning strength when everything inside me wanted to collapse. That inner fire was still there, waiting.

Leonie became my light, my daily dose of hope, my tiny miracle who unknowingly pieced me back together. Holding her, I felt the same surge of courage and energy I once felt walking through fire, a reminder that life could still be embraced, even after the darkest trials.

When her parents returned to work after COVID, it was just Leonie and me during the week. We quickly fell into our own rhythm. Our days were filled with laughter, play, and endless wardrobe changes. With my lifelong passion for fashion, I loved dressing her in different outfits—sometimes silly, sometimes fancy, always with a little flair. I recorded videos of her giggling, singing, dancing, or simply discovering the world in her own way.

She called me "Lola," which means grandma in Tagalog, and I melted every time she said it. Her other grandma, Cindi, she called "Biggie," and I loved watching the two of them together. Those names, those little rituals, rooted us in a shared love that felt unbreakable, even as the world remained unpredictable.

I was there for all her milestones: first wobbly steps, first precious words, first songs sung in that sweet, off-key toddler voice. Every moment with her felt like a gift, a reminder that beauty exists in the smallest things. She lit up my world in ways I had not imagined possible.

As she grew older, Cindi picked her up on Tuesdays, and Leonie spent the night with her. It gave me a much-needed break, yet I missed her the moment she was gone. The house felt too quiet without her laughter echoing through the rooms.

When pre-kindergarten began, a new routine emerged. I picked her up after school, and it quickly became one of my favorite parts of the day. Seeing her little face light up when she spotted me and ran into my arms was pure joy. No matter how heavy the day felt, those moments lifted me every time.

Watching Leonie grow filled the empty spaces in my heart I once believed would never heal. She brought laughter back into my world and light into rooms that had long been dim. For the first time in years, I felt truly alive. Healing does not come all at once—it arrives quietly, through small hands, bright eyes, and moments that remind you love still exists.

Even as I embraced this newfound joy, I sensed life was not finished testing me. Challenges waited just beyond the horizon, moments that would push me to my limits and demand every ounce of strength I had. I had survived kidnappings, sexual assault, heartbreak, and loss. Yet I could not shake the feeling that the next trial would be my hardest, a test that could change everything.

I held Leonie a little tighter, my heart bracing, as if I would soon need every ounce of courage and every lesson I had learned. I did not yet know that my body would betray me in a way that could leave me paralyzed, my life hanging in the balance. Every heartbeat, every step I took with Leonie in my arms, was a fragile reminder that the next chapter of survival was already waiting.

CHAPTER 48.5
THE SPACE BETWEEN

After Leonie saved my life, and God's hand steadying me through it all, I half-expected a miracle ending. It did not come. What followed was quiet, uneven, and slow. Healing did not announce itself. It crept in sideways and demanded patience I was not always sure I had.

There were days when simply waking up felt like an accomplishment. My body still felt unfamiliar, and I moved cautiously, listening for signs I might miss something again. Fear lurked in the corners of ordinary moments, whispering that if I relaxed even a little, life could slip through my fingers once more.

But there were small victories too. I started sleeping through the night without jolting awake in panic. Hunger returned, not just for food, but for ordinary pleasures: conversation, fresh air, routine. I laughed, sometimes unexpectedly, and then caught myself wondering if it was okay to feel light again after everything that had happened.

I leaned inward more than I ever had before, and outward toward my faith, not for answers, but for steadiness. I did not need certainty. I needed something to hold on to when fear crept back in, something that reminded me I was not carrying everything alone.

Over the months, my routines became pillars, holding me steady when fear crept in. My doctor appointments shifted from urgent visits to half-yearly checkups. About two years in, I gradually stopped seeing my psychologist and psychiatrist. I had learned to rely more on myself, on my faith, and on the quiet strategies I had built to keep fear at bay.

I started dating occasionally, testing the possibility of opening myself up again. I had not yet made real friends in San Diego, but instead of letting that loneliness define me, I began doing things on my own. I went to church, joined in church groups, went to the movies, and dined at restaurants. I did not think of it as going alone. I thought of it as going with myself, and surprisingly, that felt like enough.

Dance remained my constant. I found myself at Madhouse Dance four to five times a week, sometimes taking two classes in one day. Those classes were something I always looked forward to. The music, the movement, and the familiar burn in my muscles reminded me that my body was still capable, still expressive, still mine. In those hours, I stopped monitoring my body and simply let it move. I was present and alive inside my own skin.

By the third year, the darkness that had once been relentless was showing up less and less. When it appeared, I no longer felt powerless. I fought back, stood my ground, and refused to let it dictate my days—holding on to my faith in God and whispering prayers in the moments I felt myself slipping. Each time I held my ground, it felt a little easier the next time. Life was no longer about simply surviving. It was about learning to thrive, even cautiously, even imperfectly.

I was healing, yes, but that did not mean the tests were over. The quiet, ordinary days felt precious and fragile, and I cherished them fiercely. I had no idea that my body had another reckoning waiting, one that would test me in ways I could not yet imagine. For now, simply being alive felt like enough, and I clung to that fragile peace, unaware of the storm ahead.

CHAPTER 49
THE NIGHT I ALMOST DIDN'T WAKE UP

But life has a way of testing even the strongest recoveries. Just when I thought I had finally found balance again, my body threw me a curveball I never saw coming.

It was 11:30 p.m. on September 30, 2025. I got up to use the bathroom like I always did in the middle of the night. I had gone to bed early because I had an Uber scheduled for four in the morning. My flight to Puerto Vallarta was at seven, and I was not about to miss it. This was the long-awaited GF Club getaway with Yolanda, Judi, and Irma. Puerto Vallarta is my sanctuary. I go every year, sometimes twice, and I was so excited to show the girls all my favorite spots.

But that night, my body was no longer on my side.

I climbed back into bed hoping to steal a couple more hours of sleep before my 3:00 a.m. alarm. That hope lasted about thirty seconds.

The pain started in my back, sharp and sudden. It was nothing like my kidney failure pain. This was different. Worse. I repositioned, turned, curled on my side, tried lying on my stomach. Relief never came. I stood up, trying to shake it off. My mind refused to accept that anything could interfere with my trip.

The pain tightened its grip with every passing second. I tried walking and stretching, but the pain refused to relent. That is when real fear hit me. Not nerves, not anxiety, but a primal, bone-deep fear. My body was telling me something was seriously wrong.

I forced myself upstairs and knocked on my daughter's bedroom door. It was close to midnight, and the sound startled Ashley and Kris awake.

The moment Ashley opened the door, the words tumbled out of me in a broken, desperate cry.

"Ashley, can you please call me an ambulance? I am in unbearable pain. My back is killing me and it keeps getting worse."

My voice didn't even sound like mine. It was raw, high, frantic. The kind of voice that makes panic rise instantly in the person listening.

Ashley insisted on driving me herself. And she regretted that decision before we even reached the main road.

The moment we got in the car, the pain became hellish. I was screaming at the top of my lungs. Every bump, every turn, every breath sent shocks through my spine that made the world blur.

Ashley was white-knuckled behind the wheel. I could feel her panic growing with every mile. She kept repeating, "We're almost there, Mom. Hang on. We're almost there." Her voice trembled. She was trying to convince both of us.

She pulled up at the emergency room entrance and ran inside shouting for help. No one came. She rushed back out with a wheelchair and found me twisted across the back seat, unable to move. It took everything I had just to sit up and slide myself into the chair.

Finally, an attendant came out and wheeled me into the ER. Inside, the fluorescent lights felt harsh and unreal. Out of habit, I handed over my insurance card and driver's license, barely able to speak.

Answering their questions was nearly impossible. I was crying, screaming, begging for help. My voice echoed through the ER.

"Please help me, God. Please help me, please…"

I had no control. The pain was too much, too big, swallowing every part of me. It felt unnatural, punishing, like something was ripping straight through my spine. I had survived kidney failure and a collapsed heart valve, but this was worse. Much worse. The kind of pain that makes you believe you might actually die from it.

Ashley eventually made it back inside and found me still clawing through the agony. She pressed ice packs into my back, whispering to me through clenched teeth. My screams no longer sounded human; they sounded like something dying.

They gave me Dilaudid through an IV, which is stronger than morphine. Nothing. A second dose. Nothing. A third. Still nothing.

Then they brought out the Ketamine, the one they call a horse tranquilizer.

The moment it hit my veins, everything went black.

I woke up to someone insistently tapping on my chest, shouting, "Come on, Janette, wake up, wake up." Someone else tugged hard at my toes. My eyes fluttered open to a circle of faces. Doctors, nurses, techs—all hovering, all ready to jump in. I had overdosed. The cocktail of opioids and Ketamine had pushed me to the edge. My oxygen levels had plummeted. My breathing slowed. I was slipping away.

They hit me with Narcan. The drug slammed into my system, ripping the opioids from my receptors and forcing me back into consciousness. Without it, I might not have woken up at all.

Ashley was shaken to her core. She told me later that when they injected the Ketamine, my head tilted back, mouth open, tongue slack. She thought she lost me.

I went to the ER because of unbearable pain, and I almost did not come out.

When the chaos finally settled, something miraculous happened. The pain had eased. Not gone, but bearable. I could breathe again. Think again. It felt like mercy.

The doctor didn't waste a second. With the pain finally under control, they ordered a CT scan and an MRI. Honestly, if I had still been in that kind of agony, there was no way I could have stayed still for either. I would have been thrashing, crying, screaming, anything but still.

After the scans, they made the call: I was being admitted. I would be spending the night.

By then, I was no longer in severe pain, just floating in a strange in-between. Loopy. Detached. A mix of shock, exhaustion, and whatever was dripping through my IV.

I remember turning to the nurse and asking, more than once, "Is there any chance I can still make it to Puerto Vallarta?"

The answer was obvious, but in my haze I clung to that tiny spark of hope. I blamed it on the Dilaudid.

Once they wheeled me into a hospital room and got Ashley settled on a cot beside me, she immediately went into protector mode, texting, calling, updating the family—and Phil, who I had been dating for about a year. I watched her through half-closed eyes, so composed and strong even as fear sat heavy on her face.

We still did not know what was wrong, but at least the pain was no longer devouring me. That alone felt like a victory.

When I finally had the strength, I sent a text to the girls. I told them what had happened, apologized for missing the trip, and told them to go enjoy it anyway. My heart sank while writing those words. We had planned that trip all year, and now here I was, hospital gown instead of swimsuit, fluorescent lights instead of Mexican sun.

But deep down, I knew the truth. I hadn't just missed a vacation. I had narrowly escaped something far worse. Or had I?

CHAPTER 50
WAITING AND WORRY

I managed to get a few hours of sleep before the neurosurgeon came into my room. I don't think Ashley got a single minute of rest. She looked completely drained, her body present but her mind still replaying everything we had just been through.

I recognized the neurosurgeon immediately. He had treated me a few years back when I was recovering from my stroke at this same hospital. But this time, he looked different. Older. Slower. Even the way he spoke felt fragmented, like his sentences were slipping through my fingers before I could catch them.

There was no confusion, however, when he went over the MRI results.

They had found a hematoma the size of a baseball, compressing my spine. A mass of blood pressing dangerously on my spinal cord. This kind of situation calls for immediate emergency surgery. The longer you wait, the greater the risk of permanent paralysis.

Then came the twist.

There was one major obstacle. I was on blood thinners.

He said he could not perform the surgery until the medication was fully out of my system. That could take up to two weeks.

"If I operate while the blood thinners are still in your system," he said, "there is a very high chance you will bleed out on the table and will not survive."

His words hit me like a brick wall. Two weeks? I had to lie in this bed for two weeks, knowing that with every passing day I was rolling the dice with my spinal cord? The thought was unthinkable.

The next day, the attending doctor who had cared for me in the ER stopped by for rounds. He reviewed the MRI again, and Ashley and I immediately voiced our concern about waiting two weeks for surgery.

He looked surprised.

We explained what the neurosurgeon had told us. That is when he clarified. He had spoken with the same surgeon earlier that day, and apparently the plan had changed. The surgery was now scheduled for the upcoming Saturday.

We were very confused.

Later that afternoon, the neurosurgeon returned and confirmed that he would be performing the surgery on Saturday.

Ashley, still reeling, asked him directly, "What changed your mind? You told us yesterday it would take two weeks, and now it is happening in five days?"

He mumbled something vague about talking to his colleagues and doing research, clearly unwilling to dwell on it. Then he began talking about the procedure itself. He explained that he would need to remove two bones from my spine to extract the hematoma.

I asked, "What happens to the bones after that?" I was half wondering if they would put them back and screw them in place or use something artificial. I was not a doctor, just curious.

His response was short and clipped. "Then we throw them out."

No explanation. No reassurance. Just that.

I did not like this man. At all.

He had zero bedside manner, no empathy, and the personality of a brick. Later we learned he was eighty-two years old. I was not judging his skills based on age, but this would be a high-risk spinal surgery with no margin for error. From the cold, disconnected vibe he gave off, neither Ashley nor I felt confident putting my life and my spine in his hands.

So I asked my nurse if there was any way to request a different neurosurgeon. She said she would talk to the attending doctor and see what could be done.

A few hours later, she came back with an answer. Another neurosurgeon was willing to take my case and would try to stop by between surgeries.

And then he walked in.

Dr. Udani.

The moment he stepped into the room, everything changed. He introduced himself with the warmest, most genuine smile, and I immediately felt a sense of calm. Before he arrived, Ashley and I had googled him and checked his reviews. He passed with flying colors. But seeing him in person sealed it.

It was Monday when we met Dr. Udani. He said that if the blood thinners were fully out of my system, he could operate on Thursday. He was confident it could be done. Five days from my last dose of blood thinners would be enough time for them to clear my system.

For the first time since this nightmare began, I felt a sliver of hope.

That sliver did not last long.

With all the free time I had lying in that bed, I did the worst thing possible. I started reading up on my condition.

A spinal hematoma, especially one as large as mine, was not just rare. It was extremely rare. And extremely dangerous.

The danger was not only the surgery but also the waiting. Even without blood thinners, the risk was high. My medical history only complicated things further.

Operating near the spinal cord carries terrifying possibilities. Paralysis. Nerve damage. Permanent loss of function. Excessive bleeding. A second hematoma forming. And then there was the bone removal, which would weaken spinal stability and extend the time spent under anesthesia.

And anesthesia was its own beast for me.

I have a bioprosthetic valve in my heart, which means I am far more vulnerable under sedation. My heart does not have the reserve to handle drops in blood pressure. Add to that the infection risk that comes with a prosthetic valve, and the dangers multiply.

My sliver of hope quickly turned into a storm of worry.

My family was worried too. They all knew what was at stake.

My brother Jun, his wife Ingrid, and my nephew Josh planned to arrive from Northern California the day before surgery. My sister Joji and her husband Danny would come, too. My sister Jane and my brother-in-law John could not come; they were in Canada, watching their son play in the Toronto Blue Jays minor league system.

By Wednesday, my hospital room was full, alive with conversations that eased the tension just enough to breathe. Leonie visited every day after school. On her first day, she brought me a homemade get-well card covered with drawings of our hands and a monster truck. She looked up at me and said, "I made this so you feel better, Lola."

I smiled through tears. Every small word, every touch, reminded me that I was not facing this alone.

That evening, we received confirmation that the surgery was a go for the next day. My labs showed no trace of blood thinners, and Dr. Udani said everything was ready.

Still, when everyone said goodnight and left, I was alone again with the what-ifs. The spiral did not last long. I was still on medication every four hours because without it the pain would have been unbearable. Thankfully, it dulled both the agony and the fear just enough to let me sleep.

Reality hit hard the next morning. Surgery was scheduled for 4:30 p.m., which felt like torture, not only because I had to fast all day, but because of the sheer weight of waiting. There was a real chance I would not wake up from the anesthesia at all, and if I did, I might wake up paralyzed.

I prayed with everything in me. I begged God to spare me from paralysis, telling Him through tears that if that was my fate, I would rather He take my life instead. The moment the words left my heart, I felt the guilt of them. I asked Him to forgive me for even thinking it, for letting fear speak louder than faith, but in that moment I was a mother, a grandmother, a woman in unbearable pain, clinging to the only strength greater than my own.

The night before, I had gone over everything with Kristin and Ashley, the uncomfortable just in case conversation. They knew exactly what to do if I did not survive.

The nurses were especially attentive that morning, checking vitals and double checking everything.

Danny and Joji arrived shortly after noon. Everyone else was supposed to arrive around 2:30 p.m.

But just before 2:00, everything changed.

A nurse stepped into the room. "They are here for you," she said.

We all looked at each other, wide eyed. "Already?" we said together.

Yes. Already.

Panic hit me instantly.

They were taking me early. I wasn't ready. The rest of my family wasn't there yet. I hadn't said my final goodbyes.

Danny and Joji walked beside me as far as they were allowed. When they had to stop, I turned my head toward them. My throat tightened. "This is it," I said through tears. "I love you guys."

It was not supposed to happen like this.

As the gurney rolled forward, the prayers started in my head. Please, God, do not let me wake up paralyzed. Please do not let me lose the ability to walk. And in that moment, gripped by fear, a darker thought flickered through me once again—a fear so heavy it made me question everything I thought I was strong enough to face.

Joji and I had already talked about that. If I did not make it through, she would finish my memoir. This memoir is more than just a story. It carries *my* story. A legacy. A message for people like me who have endured, survived, and kept going. My life matters. My story matters. And in that moment, I prayed for the chance to keep telling it.

They wheeled me into the pre-op room, and suddenly everything felt clinical, quiet, and painfully real. A nurse introduced herself in a steady, practiced voice that somehow calmed me. She explained every step of what would happen next, and her certainty gave me the smallest sense of safety.

The anesthesiologist arrived soon after. She explained the delicate balance required because of my prosthetic heart valve. Too much anesthesia could be dangerous. But she spoke with confidence, and when her eyes met mine, I believed she would protect me.

Two attendants came in and explained that the IV would be placed in my upper arm because they would start with me face down and later turn me onto my side. I nodded, absorbing their words even as my thoughts raced ahead into the unknown.

Then Dr. Udani walked in.

He greeted me with the same warm smile that had comforted me since the moment we met. He marked my spine with careful precision, a quiet ritual that felt almost sacred. Before he stepped away, he rested a hand gently near my shoulder and said, "Everything is going to go well."

Something inside me loosened.

When they wheeled me toward the operating room, another team of staff members waited inside, fully suited and ready. Each one introduced themselves with kindness in their voices and reassurance in their eyes. Their presence chipped away at my fear, softening the edges of my panic. Something in me eased, and I did not feel alone.

They prepared to move me from the gurney to the operating table. I braced myself to count backwards from ten, the familiar ritual I had rehearsed in my mind. It had always given me a small sense of control.

But this time, I never got the chance.

The world fell away before I could say a single number.

Blackness.

Silence.

Nothing.

CHAPTER 51
I CAN MOVE

And suddenly, I opened my eyes. A bright, sterile light glowed faintly above me. I was in a different room now. Everything was a little blurry, as if I were underwater. I blinked, trying to get my bearings, and saw a nurse leaning over me, quietly checking my vitals. Her expression was calm and composed.

Still dazed, I croaked out the only question I could manage. "When are they going to operate?"

She looked down at me with a warm, almost maternal smile and said softly, "Oh, you're all done, honey. And you did great."

Done?

It didn't register at first. My brain was still trying to connect the dots. I hadn't counted backwards. I hadn't felt anything. There was no memory of being transferred from the gurney to the operating table. One minute I had been bracing for the unknown, and the next thing I knew, I was waking up here.

And then it hit me. If the surgery was over, could I move from the waist down?

I held my breath. Slowly, cautiously, I wiggled my toes.

They moved.

I rotated my ankles. First the right, then the left.

They moved.

I lifted one leg, then the other.

They moved.

A wave of relief crashed over me. It was so powerful it almost took my breath away.

I could move. I could feel. I was not paralyzed.

Tears welled in my eyes. *Hallelujah. Praise Jesus. Thank you, God.*

I prayed silently, over and over, my lips barely moving while my soul shouted the words. I had survived. And not just survived. I had made it through what I feared most with my body whole. I could hardly believe it.

But then, I did.

Lying under those bright lights with the monitors softly beeping, I felt the power of prayer in a way I never had before. Family, relatives, friends, friends of friends, entire prayer groups had taken my name and lifted it to heaven. In the days before surgery, my phone had filled with messages that carried so much love and faith. Hard, strong prayers sent like lifelines across distance. I had read every one, sometimes over and over, absorbing them like oxygen when fear tightened around me.

And now here I was. Awake. Moving. Whole.

Just hours earlier, I had begged God not to let me wake up paralyzed. I had accepted that I might not wake up at all. I had said my goodbyes. I had prepared my daughters to handle my affairs in case the worst happened.

I had stared death, and the possibility of permanent disability, straight in the face. And now here I was. Alive. Awake. Whole.

The surgery was behind me.

I knew there was still a long road ahead with recovery, pain management, and physical therapy, but this moment was its own miracle. A quiet, unassuming miracle tucked between fading anesthesia and the beeping of machines. One I would never forget.

As they wheeled me toward my new room, still groggy but fully aware, I asked the nurse, "When will my family be able to see me?"

"Right away," she answered.

I followed up quickly. "Is there a limit to how many people can come in?"

"No limit at all," she said.

"Even my four-year-old granddaughter?"

"Absolutely."

Wow. I remembered the old days when only one or two visitors were allowed and usually only immediate family. The thought of having everyone around me so soon brought a wave of comfort.

When they brought me into my room in the west wing, I was stunned. It was huge, more like a private suite than a hospital room. Spacious, bright, and surprisingly comfortable. It didn't feel cold or bleak. It felt welcoming.

At first, the room was empty. Because I had gone into surgery earlier than scheduled, there had been some confusion about where I had been moved afterward. Eventually the messages reached my daughters, and little by little, everyone began making their way over.

At first, just a couple of family members tiptoed inside, whispering softly. The rest stayed in the hallway, assuming they had to take turns. I waved them in and said, "It's okay. Everyone is allowed in."

That was all it took.

Within minutes, the room filled up.

They brought in all the flowers from my previous room along with fresh bouquets. The suite transformed before my eyes. It no longer looked like a hospital room. It looked alive. Cozy and bright, overflowing with color, laughter, and love.

I asked for my phone and opened the front-facing camera to take a quick look at myself. I expected to see someone swollen and exhausted, a woman who had just come out of spinal surgery.

Instead, I was shocked. I looked good. Lively, even.

A nurse named Monica came in to introduce herself. She glanced at me and said, "Wow, you look great."

I smiled. "Thank you. Yes, I do, don't I?"

Because I felt it. No pain. No fog. Just presence. And if I am being honest, a little amazement.

I had been so fortunate with every nurse who came through, even during shift changes. Each one was warm, attentive, and genuinely kind. I bonded with several of them. They weren't distant or cold. They treated me like a real person.

By evening, my room was packed. A dozen loved ones gathered around me: my family—Joji, Danny, Jun, Ingrid, Josh, Kristin, Ryan, Ashley, and precious little Leonie; Ashley's in-laws, Iraj and Cindi; and Phil. He had been there every night during my two-and-a-half-week hospital stay. The room hummed with noise and joy, and surrounded by them, a sense of peace settled in my heart.

There was so much talking and laughing. Leonie flew through the air in her dad's arms, giggling like she could really soar. We were probably far too loud for a hospital.

Monica walked in again, smiling at the chaos.

"Oops. Are we being too noisy? Is everyone getting kicked out?" I asked nervously.

She shook her head. "Absolutely not. I just wanted to see what all the fun was about."

And that was pretty amazing.

After everything I had endured, here I was. Alive. Intact. Wrapped in laughter, love, and life.

In that room, surrounded by the love of everyone I held dear, I felt completely whole. Every breath, every heartbeat, every glance at my family reminded me that I had truly survived—not just the surgery, not just the fear, not just the darkness of my past. I had survived it all, and through it every step of the way, I knew God had never left my side.

EPILOGUE

Looking back on the twists and turns of my life, from childhood shadows to the challenges of adulthood, I realized how far I had come. I had survived. Not just the surgeries, kidnappings, heartbreak, or depression, but the long journey from the girl I once was to the woman I had become. I had emerged whole because I chose to rise.

The girl who once felt ugly, irrelevant, and unloved grew into a woman who finally turned toward her shadows and said, Enough. Leonie gave me the push to stop running, but the healing came from my choice to face my demons, leaning on prayer and trusting that God was guiding me through it.

As we grew into adulthood, my siblings and I became more than family. We became friends, confidants, and anchors for one another. My parents, in their own imperfect ways, loved me too. Understanding that now does not erase the past, but it allows me to carry it without bitterness.

I have weathered storms, including a failed marriage, kidnappings, heart surgery, a stroke, depression, and a spinal hematoma. Each dark, tangled thread wove a story of resilience, courage, and growth, teaching me that even the deepest shadows cannot dim the light we choose to nurture.

Being surrounded by my daughters, my granddaughter Leonie, and the people who prayed for me reminded me that happiness is not the absence of pain. It is the decision to stay, to live, and to connect, even when shadows linger.

I wrote this memoir to honor the truth. Even in our darkest moments, choice, hope, light, and love remain.

The darkness still whispers, but I no longer fear it. Even when it tried to tap me on the shoulder after I came home from the hospital, I rose above it, stepping into life with determination and joy. It was challenging to adjust to my new limits, but I stayed committed and positive, focused on regaining my strength. My immediate goal was simple: get back to Mad House and keep dancing. Exactly three months after my surgery, I stepped back into the studio, and I have been dancing ever since, continuing to move through life with courage, joy, and determination, no matter what challenges come my way.

AFTERWORD

Writing this memoir has reminded me of the strength we often don't realize we carry until we are tested. Every fear faced, every heartbreak endured, every small victory led me here.

Life will challenge you. You can rise, you can heal, and you can continue to dance through joy, sorrow, and everything in between. Keep dancing and let every step forward be a celebration of the light you choose to carry.

STAY CONNECTED

Thank you for walking this journey with me.

If *The Long Dance Back* spoke to you, I'd love to hear from you.

Instagram:
@janettemari.author

Email:
janettemari.author@gmail.com

If you feel led to leave a brief review on Amazon or Goodreads, it would mean so much—and help this story reach others who may need it.

Keep dancing,

www.ingramcontent.com/pod-product-compliance
Ingram Content Group UK Ltd.
Pitfield, Milton Keynes, MK11 3LW, UK
UKHW040242300726
14061UKWH00002BD/119